THE UNDERGRADUATE EXPERIENCE

THE UNDERGRADUATE EXPERIENCE

FOCUSING INSTITUTIONS ON WHAT MATTERS MOST

Peter Felten
John N. Gardner
Charles C. Schroeder
Leo M. Lambert
Betsy O. Barefoot

JB JOSSEY-BASS™
A Wiley Brand

Published by Jossey-Bass
A Wiley Brand
One Montgomery Street, Suite 1000, San Francisco, CA 94104-4594—www.josseybass.com

Jossey-Bass books and products are available through most bookstores. To contact Jossey-Bass directly call our Customer Care Department within the U.S. at 800-956-7739, outside the U.S. at 317-572-3986, or fax 317-572-4002.

Wiley publishes in a variety of print and electronic formats and by print-on-demand. Some material included with standard print versions of this book may not be included in e-books or in print-on-demand. If this book refers to media such as a CD or DVD that is not included in the version you purchased, you may download this material at http://booksupport.wiley.com. For more information about Wiley products, visit www.wiley.com.

Library of Congress Cataloging-in-Publication Data available at:

ISBN 978-1-119-05074-2 (Hardcover)
ISBN 978-1-119-05122-0 (ePDF)
ISBN 978-1-119-05119-0 (ePub)

Cover design by Wiley
Cover image: ©Macduff Everton/Getty Images, Inc. and ©AlinaMD/iStockphoto

Printed in the United States of America

FIRST EDITION

HB Printing 10 9 8 7 6 5 4 3

CONTENTS

FOREWORD

COLLEGE AND UNIVERSITY LEADERS WHO SEEK TO ENHANCE the student experience will find this book especially uplifting because the authors are leaders in their own right, with deep experience and success in setting visions, developing plans, and reaching goals. These are can-do, get-it-done educators.

Even more important, the authors are leaders who understand that moving a college or university forward is not about one person but rather about a community and the culture of the institution. In fact, what comes through as one reads the illustrations in this book and absorbs their lessons is that the substance of an institution's culture is particularly critical to what we can achieve. Many institutions talk about supporting all students and about being mission driven. However, institutions that are most effective are those that foster broad agreement on priorities, allow people to ask questions and take initiative, and offer incentives and rewards to those who innovate.

The book provides excellent examples of colleges and universities staying true to their missions—continually evolving and innovating to ensure success in those missions. In fact, the authors place "positive restlessness" at the center of successful institutional leadership. This is the notion, outlined by George Kuh and colleagues in 2010, that one must be constantly seeking and striving to improve, determined not to be satisfied and not to say, "Been there, done that." On my campus, my colleagues constantly remark that success is never final. We use data analytics and focus groups to gather deep information on issues that arise; ask difficult questions about our assumptions and the data; involve faculty, staff, and students in these conversations; and develop strategies that are critical to constant improvement.

Some readers may be bothered by the book authors' assertion that money is not everything. Yet many will be convinced by the argument that although funding is always necessary, its even more important to make the best use of those funds and to think carefully about the priorities that must be protected. It really is true that during times of scarcity, enlightened institutions can become more imaginative in their spending. The question is, what are the priorities that are most critical to carrying out the mission of the institution? The book addresses the fundamental question of how to use funds not just to make incremental changes but also to transform the institution in ways that can be sustained.

It is sometimes very easy for leaders to become discouraged by forces beyond their control, whether by trends in state and federal policies and funding or the demands of boards, elected officials, and alumni. For leaders who find themselves discouraged because of external constituents and forces, the authors argue that the focus must be on controlling the things that we have the power to control, starting with the work we do to carry out our fundamental missions: promoting student learning and ensuring the quality of the student experience. They argue that leaders at multiple levels have a major impact on the quality of the undergraduate experience—especially if they pay attention to students, understand their backgrounds, and align the culture of the institution with the students it serves.

They also go beyond the typical discussion involving retention and graduation rates to challenge us to focus on the undergraduate experience. Of course, like money, retention and completion are very important, but the authors are correct that the essence of education is about more than keeping students in college. It is about learning how to learn, asking good questions, analyzing data and information, putting whatever is going on in the world into perspective, and making sound, informed decisions.

Each chapter provides examples that bring these issues to life and give them new meaning. Educators often talk about caring about all students. This book is different because it acknowledges that one-size-fits-all strategies for learning seldom work, yet that certain principles of learning can be applied effectively to meet the needs of all students from all backgrounds at all types of institutions. Here is where the authors deliver at the very practical level. For example, they note the challenges students face when they lack the financial resources to participate in enriching extracurricular experiences, such as study abroad programs. Readers will find the practical discussion of linking budgets with priorities especially helpful as a means for supporting students and institutions.

Leaders—present and future—interested in enhancing the student experience will be challenged to think about their own visions and goals in relation to strategic planning, developing priorities, budgeting, and other institutional functions. The authors also address a number of other critical leadership issues, including strengthening communication across campus and nurturing relationships among key constituents of the institution. One essential characteristic of a healthy institutional culture is the extent to which the climate encourages transparency and honest dialogue. The very meaning of shared governance involves cooperation and collaboration among the different groups at the institution.

These authors—and the institutions they represent—understand that what we do in higher education will have a profound impact on our students and the future of our country, whether we are talking about social justice or economic well-being. In essence, the authors inspire us to think about our own institutions, leadership styles, and visions, with the hope that these stories can strengthen our resolve to change and turn our visions into the desired reality.

Most important, they offer optimism at a time when we need it more than ever. Every generation in higher education has faced challenges and opportunities, and so do we. We face a globalizing social and economic context, shifting fiscal politics, changing demographics, accelerating technological change, and advances in teaching and learning. I often tell my students that the way we think about ourselves, the language that we use, and the values that we hold shape who we become. We hear an increasing number of people predicting a gloomy future for higher education. If we are not careful, that gloomy picture will become reality. This book offers us—through both hope and evidence of success—a positive vision to which we can all aspire. Our students need us and this vision now more than ever.

Freeman A. Hrabowski III
President, University of Maryland, Baltimore County

ACKNOWLEDGMENTS

MANY COLLEAGUES HAVE INSPIRED AND TAUGHT US throughout our careers. Two merit particular attention here: Russell Edgerton and George Keller. As president of the American Association for Higher Education and then as a senior program officer for higher education at The Pew Charitable Trusts, Edgerton mentored and profoundly influenced us as individuals and academics. From his perch at the University of Pennsylvania, the late George Keller was a preeminent scholar and advisor to higher education who shaped how we understand our work and our institutions. We are deeply indebted to both of them.

Pat Hutchings, Lou Albert, and Gerry Francis gave us invaluable feedback on an earlier version of this manuscript. Megan Scribner, Laura St. Cyr, and Sandra Fields provided editorial guidance along the way, and Alyx Bean served as editorial assistant. Jessica Pasion kept us organized and well fed. The Elon School of Law hosted our meetings, allowing us to focus on what matters most.

And while John Gardner and Betsy Barefoot had the pleasure of collaborating on this project as a husband and wife team, the spouses of Peter, Charles, and Leo (Sara Walker, Barbara Schroeder, and Laurie Lambert) have been wonderfully supportive and patient with us as we have focused on this project.

ABOUT THE AUTHORS

THE FIVE COAUTHORS OF THIS VOLUME BRING DIFFERENT perspectives on undergraduate education. Collectively we have worked in a wide range of institutions, from public community colleges to private research universities. We have consulted on hundreds of different campuses, served as staff and faculty in roles from assistant professor to dean and president, been elected to leadership roles in diverse professional associations, contributed to the scholarship of higher education, and edited several higher education journals. In this book we aim to distill what we have learned from those many experiences.

So that you know a bit about each of us, we will introduce ourselves briefly:

Peter Felten is assistant provost for teaching and learning and professor of history at Elon University. He also is the executive director of the Center for Engaged Learning, which sponsors multi-institutional research on high-impact practices, and the Center for the Advancement of Teaching and Learning, which coordinates faculty development at Elon. His recent publications include the coauthored books *Transforming Students: Fulfilling the Promise of Higher Education* (Johns Hopkins University Press, 2014) and *Engaging Students as Partners in Learning and Teaching* (Jossey-Bass, 2014). He is a former president of the Professional and Organizational Development (POD) Network and currently is president-elect of the International Society of the Scholarship of Teaching and Learning. He coedits the *International Journal for Academic Development*, a leading journal for faculty and organizational developers in higher education.

John N. Gardner is president (and cofounder in 1999 with Betsy O. Barefoot) of the John N. Gardner Institute for Excellence in Undergraduate Education, a nonprofit corporation that partners with all types of postsecondary institutions to improve student success. He is also senior fellow and distinguished professor emeritus at the University of South Carolina (USC). A leading expert on the first-year experience and high-impact practices in undergraduate education, Gardner was the founding executive director at USC of both the widely replicated University 101 course from 1974 to 1999 and the National Resource Center for The First-Year Experience and Students in Transition from 1986 to 1999, the host of the popular annual conference on The First-Year Experience. One of the most prolific scholars of American higher education, Gardner has written about and developed interventions to improve the success of other undergraduate populations, especially sophomores, transfers, and seniors. In recognition of his contributions, he is the recipient of 12 honorary degrees, including from his employer of three decades, the University of South Carolina, where much earlier in his career he was awarded the university's outstanding teaching award.

Charles Schroeder is one of the nation's leading student affairs administrators, having served as chief student affairs officer at the Georgia Institute of Technology, Mercer

University, Saint Louis University, and the University of Missouri-Columbia, where he also was a full professor in the Department of Educational Leadership and Policy Analysis. He has published more than 85 articles and books on higher education, including the coedited volume *Realizing the Educational Potential of Residence Halls* (Jossey-Bass, 1994). He was the founder and first executive editor of *About Campus: Enriching the Student Learning Experience*, a journal published bimonthly by Wiley and ACPA-College Student Educators International. He also was part of the 12-member study group that drafted *Principles of Good Practices for Student Affairs*, published by ACPA and NASPA. Schroeder has served two terms as president of the American College Personnel Association and received both the Esther Lloyd-Jones Professional Service Award and the Contributions to Knowledge Award from that organization. Schroeder currently provides consulting services to a range of colleges and universities.

Leo M. Lambert is in his eighteenth year as president of Elon University. He has advanced two ambitious strategic plans to establish Elon as a premier liberal arts university. Elon's enrollment has grown by 40% since Lambert arrived in 1999, and the university has earned accolades as one of the most productive campuses for both Fulbright graduates and Peace Corps volunteers. During his tenure, Elon has added new schools of law and health sciences, constructed 100 new buildings, begun a major initiative to develop the residential campus, and earned Phi Beta Kappa status. Lambert has been a champion for college access, establishing Elon's Center for Access and Success and the Elon Academy. He has also been a proponent of multifaith initiatives at the university, including the construction of the Numen

Lumen Pavilion, Elon's multifaith center. During his career, he has been active on the boards of the Association of American Colleges and Universities, Campus Compact, North Carolina Campus Compact, the American Association for Higher Education, and the National Association of Independent Colleges and Universities, and also on committees of the NCAA.

Betsy O. Barefoot is a prominent scholar of higher education, having served for 11 years as the codirector for research and publications in the National Resource Center for The First-Year Experience and Students in Transition at the University of South Carolina. As noted already, she is the cofounder of the John N. Gardner Institute for Excellence in Undergraduate Education, and she serves as its senior scholar. Barefoot has co-authored a number of publications, including the 2005 Jossey-Bass books *Achieving and Sustaining Institutional Excellence for the First Year of College* and *Challenging and Supporting the First-Year Student: A Handbook for the First Year of College*. She has also edited *The First Year and Beyond: Rethinking the Challenge of Collegiate Transition*, a 2008 volume of *New Directions for Higher Education*. Currently, she serves as coeditor for the *New Directions for Higher Education* series. She has also served as a consultant to more than 100 college and universities in the United States and internationally.

INTRODUCTION

IN 2004, PROFESSOR GEORGE KELLER OF THE UNIVERSITY of Pennsylvania wrote a short volume that focused on Elon University, *Transforming a College: The Story of a Little-Known College's Strategic Climb to National Distinction* (Johns Hopkins University Press). Keller believed there was a dearth of good case study literature that could inform change across the American higher education landscape. He aimed to write an accessible volume about institutional transformation that could be read on a flight from New York to Chicago. The first edition was printed many times, in part to fulfill requests for bulk orders—entire boards of trustees and college faculties used the book as a common reading and then applied Keller's ideas and lessons to their own contexts. Seven years after Keller's passing in 2007, the editorial staff of Johns Hopkins University Press asked Elon's president, Leo M. Lambert, to write a new foreword and a substantial afterword for a second edition, bringing the story up to date with Elon's 125th anniversary celebration in 2014.

Elon University has been a connecting factor in the writing of this volume as well. Two of the authors (Felten and Lambert) are Elon faculty members and administrators, two are the parent and stepparent of a 1998 alumnus (Gardner and

Barefoot), and Schroeder has been a close friend and advisor to the institution.

While Keller focused heavily on the question of strategy— how to move an institution forward dramatically given finite resources—the authors of the present volume ask a different pair of questions: What matters most in the undergraduate experience? What is possible when colleges and universities focus on what matters most?

This volume differs from Keller's in another important way. Rather than restrict the scope of this examination to one case study or a limited set of institutions, this volume highlights examples of good practice from colleges and universities across the spectrum of U.S. higher education, both public and private and large and small and ranging from the highly selective to those with open access.

Given the wide variety of institutions and students in higher education, we must envision the undergraduate experience broadly. According to the National Center for Education Statistics, some 17.3 million students enrolled as undergraduates in the United States in fall 2015; nearly half of those were enrolled at two-year institutions. The majority of students in American higher education are under age 25 years, but more than 40% are older than that. Today's undergraduates vary in a wide range of other important ways, too, including race and ethnicity, socioeconomic status, and educational background. And these students attend a rich array of institutions, from community colleges to research universities, from residential campuses to fully online institutions, and from liberal arts colleges to technical institutes. This diversity profoundly shapes both an individual student's undergraduate experience, in and beyond the curriculum, and the mission and scope of a college or university. Despite that variation, in this book we will argue that certain core themes are essential for all undergraduate students and institutions.

We chose to profile certain programs and institutions based on our own experiences and on the scholarly literature. We also looked for models of excellence that could be replicated at different types of institutions, with a bias toward those that have well-established outcomes and that do not require vast resources to sustain. Indeed, we sought to find what the surgeon and author Atul Gawande (2007) calls "the positive deviance idea—the idea of building on capabilities people already had rather than telling them how they had to change" (p. 25).

Our Hopes for This Book

As you read this book, we hope you will approach our themes and examples with your mind tuned toward positive deviance. The institutions and programs you will read about may differ substantially from your own. You may well not want to do precisely what they are doing, but we encourage you to reflect on the issues and practices in your own particular context. If you think critically and creatively, we are confident that you will be able to identify positive steps forward that work for your distinct situation and discover allies who are moving in the same direction.

As was the case with the Keller volume, we hope that this book will be read and discussed by institutional teams of faculty, staff, administrators, alumni, students, trustees, and community partners. We also hope that as a reader, you will pause at the end of each chapter, wrestle with the questions we pose, and discuss with colleagues how undergraduate education might be reimagined in ways both big and small in your own role and at your institution.

Accessing This Book's Online Materials

We have created a website to support your use of this book for retreats, courses, and discussions. On that site you will find resources you may use including print-ready hand-outs and presentation-ready slides with the Core Themes, Action Principles, and Questions for Reflection. The site also has short video interviews that elaborate on the book, and other helpful resources.

www.TheUndergraduateExperience.org

THE
UNDERGRADUATE
EXPERIENCE

1

WHAT MATTERS MOST

R ecent books on higher education typically begin by playing a variation on a familiar tune. Students are adrift. Institutions are underperforming and are also turning students into smart but soulless sheep. Colleges are in need of fundamental redesign. Financial models are in disarray. Technological disruptions are on the horizon, or perhaps the revolution is already here. Two recent book titles frame the situation simply: Is *American Higher Education in Crisis?* (Blumenstyk, 2015). No, things are worse than that because we are witnessing *The End of College* (Carey, 2015).

Although the problems facing higher education are serious, this narrative of peril and constraint obscures something crucial: Excellence abounds at colleges and universities, and not just at the most elite institutions. Looking across the landscape of higher education, we see many instances of effective practices and powerful outcomes. Undergraduates are learning, faculty and staff are working together toward aspirational goals, programs are meeting evolving needs, institutional fundamentals are stable, and the future looks bright. Although the headlines may tell a different story, in many places higher education is flourishing.

This book analyzes the common characteristics of diverse programs and institutions that are successfully navigating the challenges facing higher education. A close look at such schools highlights the promise of college while it also raises fundamental questions about the practices and purposes of undergraduate education today and tomorrow:

- The Stella and Charles Guttman Community College, the newest collegiate part of the City University of New York (CUNY), was created to enact the best research-based practices on student learning and success. Although Guttman's aim is appealing, it must pursue that goal in an environment layered with complex regulations, funding restrictions, strict labor practices, and other factors that have derailed many well-intended educational initiatives. Guttman raises the question of whether excellent undergraduate education for all students can be the central organizing principle today. Are we in higher education capable of significantly changing our practices and our institutions to meet this goal?

- Georgetown University, a global research university in Washington, D.C., that differs in nearly every way from Guttman, since 2013 has been systematically exploring a surprisingly similar question: Is it possible to design a research university "that would have liberal education values at its center but be appropriate for the world of 2030 and beyond" (Georgetown University, 2015)? In other words, how can today's undergraduate education evolve to meet the needs of students and communities in the future?

- The University of Maryland, Baltimore County (UMBC) graduates more African-American undergraduates who go on to earn PhDs in science, technology, engineering, and math (STEM) fields than any other predominantly white university in the country. UMBC's Meyerhoff Scholars Program is central to those results. For nearly three decades, this program has provided a comprehensive set of challenges to and supports for its students (Summers & Hrabowksi, 2006). The results are unparalleled. The consistent success of Meyerhoff students raises a disquieting question for other higher education institutions: If UMBC can prepare traditionally underserved students for academic success, why are so many other institutions struggling to reach that same goal?

· The University of Texas at El Paso (UTEP), a comprehensive university of more than 23,000 students, has returned to the roots of U.S. public colleges and universities to focus on enhancing students' social mobility through its high-quality programs. UTEP's story prompts us to ask whether all higher education institutions can and should address persistent social, economic, environmental, and other challenges in our communities and across our world. What is the role of undergraduate education in addressing the most pressing concerns of our students and our planet?

· Elon University in North Carolina is a private, primarily undergraduate institution of 6,500 students that over the past three decades has grown from a regional institution of fewer than 4,000 students to one that attracts 80% of its students from out of state and has dramatically enhanced its academic profile. Elon's story raises challenging questions for leaders in higher education: If this institution was able to transform itself profoundly, why have so many other colleges and universities not changed in meaningful ways? What does it take to transform a college and then to sustain and build even further on that transformation?

· Arizona State University, the largest research university in the nation, is exploring the boundaries of time and place in undergraduate education by simultaneously rooting some academic programs in specific local communities and environments while launching others online to enable students from anywhere to learn at their own convenience. Arizona State is asking important questions about when and where excellent education can happen. How do time and place matter in undergraduate education?

· Governors State University (GSU), a 5,500-student public institution in Illinois, began by offering only upper-division courses and programs. Now GSU has launched a new model for the first two years of the collegiate experience by building a curriculum and learning spaces that are linked to three central themes: civic engagement, global citizenship, and sustainability. GSU aims toward a truly integrated undergraduate education. Can higher education be more than a collection of individual credits and experiences? Is the value of a degree more than the sum of its parts?

Core Themes

Although these institutions differ in many ways, they share a common set of commitments to what matters most in the undergraduate experience. We have grouped these into six core themes.

Learning matters

The preeminent purpose of undergraduate education is student learning. Learning must be at the heart of an institution's work and at the top of its priorities. However, at the most effective colleges and universities, students are not the only ones learning—the institution itself is a learning organization. Individuals and groups in all roles at the institution, from students and front-line staff members to faculty and administrators, see themselves as active learners. They strive to question assumptions, inquire into the effectiveness of their work, partner with peers to solve problems, and make evidence-informed decisions. Effective institutions have practices and policies deliberately designed to foster learning by everyone on campus, recognizing that faculty and staff must continually learn so that they can help students to learn. More than anything else in higher education, learning matters.

Relationships matter

Student–faculty, student–staff, and student–student relationships are essential to the undergraduate experience. For a college or university to sustain excellence, however, other structural relationships also matter a great deal, such as those between academic affairs and student affairs, between student success initiatives and the faculty, between the governing board and senior administrators, and between alumni and the college. A vibrant and inclusive community emerges from the quality of the relationships that undergird it. Strong institutions value strong relationships, and they do not leave these to chance. Relationships are cultivated and nurtured intentionally at all levels.

Expectations matter

Clear and high expectations are central to the value and impact of an institution. Not only is this the case for student learning in academic courses, but it also holds true beyond the classroom. Thriving institutions have a sharp focus on the excellence of the entire student experience, including everything from admissions and financial aid processes to graduation and alumni affairs. These expectations are communicated clearly and consistently, touching everyone from prospective students and employees to experienced staff and faculty. Since such expectations both create and sustain a college or university's culture, it is especially critical to intentionally set expectations as new students, faculty, staff, and board members join the institution.

Alignment matters

Strong institutions align their resources, policies, and practices with their educational purposes and student characteristics, just as well designed courses align goals and assessments. While this may sound self-evident, it can be vexing because higher education institutions often operate as collections of strong but separate programs. Thriving institutions transform silos into systems by supporting cross-unit coordination and by paying more attention to the student experience than to how the organizational chart divides up the campus.

Improvement matters

Excellent institutions critically assess student progress and their own effectiveness on specific, relevant measures, and then use the results of that process to help students deepen their learning and faculty and staff to make improvements in their programs. The nature and quality of those outcomes should be directly connected to an institution's mission and a student's goals.

Leadership matters

In strong institutions, leaders at all levels share a sense of vision and purpose. Those at the top of the organizational chart are crucial actors, but colleges and universities cannot thrive over the long term when a single person or a small group carries a disproportionate share of the load. Instead, people throughout the organization need to see themselves as part of the leadership team. This requires everyone to work together to nurture an institutional culture of inclusion, intentionality, and purpose.

We believe that these six themes provide a heuristic, a flexible framework, for focusing both individual and institutional attention on what matters most in undergraduate education. A heuristic like this is intended not to be perfect but rather to be a tool that is useful and provocative in many contexts.

As you read, we invite and encourage you to use these themes to analyze your own and your institution's success at focusing on what matters most, adapting the framework and the examples to fit your situation. To help you in this process, we have created action principles and questions for you to consider for each of the themes. These are part of each chapter and also appear together in Appendices A and B. We hope you will use these for both personal reflection and discussions with colleagues. Doing so will enable you to come up with ideas that will work for you and your institution and enable you to move closer to your goals.

We Already Have Most of What We Need

Colleges and universities have many assets they can employ to confront the challenges facing higher education. Two particularly important factors prime colleges and universities for positive change:

First, our institutions are full of creative and smart people, and we are surrounded by many alumni, trustees, parents, and others who support our missions and who can help us see both our assets and our weaknesses. On our campuses, faculty and staff not only have expertise in their areas of specialization but also bring analytical mindsets and, often, deep experiences in problem solving, communication, and systematic action. Students also regularly refresh our institutions with new perspectives and passions. More than perhaps any other type of organization, higher education institutions have within them the human capital necessary to navigate complex challenges.

Second, although research on learning in college continues to evolve, we now know quite a lot about what contributes most to positive student outcomes. This emerging research suggests that not only are certain pedagogies and practices effective with traditional college students but also that they often are even more effective with students who have been historically disadvantaged on college campuses. And, conversely, scholars have shown that educational practices designed to support struggling undergraduates have strongly positive results for all students. In other words, despite the diversity of higher education institutions, evidence is increasingly clear about the central characteristics of effective undergraduate education. Our challenge is no longer simply to ascertain what it is we need to do; our challenge now is to do it, to create and sustain excellent undergraduate education for all of our students. That can happen only if we deliberately plan and act in ways that leverage both human capital and the research on higher education.

Building on these and other assets, we can meet our students' evolving needs by using our resources in service of what matters most. Sometimes that will involve doing new things; sometimes it will require us to stop doing something that has become our custom but is no longer effective. Sometimes it will mean doing more with less, what Schroeder (2013) calls "doing less with less—but well" (p. 46). And sometimes we will need to hang on to vital and effective parts of our work, even if they seem to be out of fashion. The path ahead does not necessarily require a radical change of course but individuals and institutions will need to make hard choices to focus limited time and resources on what matters most to the undergraduate experience.

Isolated actions, no matter how effective or purposeful, are not enough. Instead, a college needs a shared, aspirational vision for both student learning and for the institution's future. Schools have mission statements and strategic plans, but too often these do not animate the work of individuals or groups across campus. To thrive, everyone at the institution needs to be asking, how does my work contribute positively to our students' learning?

That may seem a straightforward question for faculty and staff, yet it often goes unspoken on many campuses. And for some at our institutions, such as employees in the accounting office or in the building and grounds department, that question might seem bewildering. Colleagues might ask, how could I contribute to the educational mission of the institution if I only talk to students about their tuition bills or take care of campus facilities? From a student's perspective, however, *everyone* at the institution matters. If a student is worried about whether her tuition check has cleared or if the leak in her residence hall room is fixed, she may struggle to concentrate in the classroom. Our students' education is a shared responsibility for all of us on campus.

Higher education institutions have the basic resources and the human capital necessary to be successful. Too often people within our institutions lack an aspirational vision of the possible, the will to act in purposeful yet sometimes difficult ways, and the skills to partner with others to create and fulfill that common vision. This book aims to help you and your colleagues develop the shared vision, focused will, and nimble skills necessary to do the transformational work of higher education.

Visions of the Possible

Change is hard. Sometimes it seems impossible. Individuals and institutions may have well-worn defenses to resist reform: We tried something like that before, and it didn't work; we don't have the money or the people to bring about change; we need more information before we can act; none of our peer institutions is doing something like that. The list of time-tested conversation stoppers goes on and on. As you read this book, we encourage you to focus on what is possible for you, your students, and your institution—to ask what if rather than to immediately conclude that you can't or that your institution won't because....

Constraints are real, of course. Funding is a profound challenge at many colleges and universities. When adjusted for inflation, state appropriations for higher education have been essentially flat since 1990 and have actually declined by more than 15% since 2007 (Baum & Ma, 2014). This has shifted much of the cost of higher education from states to students, contributing to real concerns about college affordability. Private institutions also have struggled as the rate of tuition increases slowed while endowments plunged during the Great Recession (Bowen, 2013). With no end to financial limits in sight, institutions have been forced to rethink priorities and practices. Although this is not easy, a scarcity of resources can provoke a new urgency and clarity of vision, prompting institutions to be more imaginative and creative in making programmatic investments (Radjou & Prabhu, 2014). In a nutshell, money matters, but it isn't everything.

Performance metrics also are an increasingly important factor in higher education decision making, particularly at public institutions. Thirty-two states currently allocate a portion of higher education funding based on indicators such as course completion rates and time to degree. Close attention to the investment of public and private funds, including tuition dollars, is essential; however, incomplete or inappropriate metrics direct students and institutions away from the most important academic, civic, and, yes, economic purposes of the academy (Delbanco, 2012). Retention rates and time to degree, for instance, are important means when evaluating an institution, but surely they are not the proper ends of undergraduate education.

Decades ago, Alexander Astin (1984) provided a useful framework for understanding the relationship among important student and institutional factors in his I-E-O theory of involvement. The outcomes (O) of a college are produced by the interaction between the inputs (I) and the environment (E). An institution typically cannot significantly change its inputs, such as the characteristics of its incoming students or the financial resources available. However, the faculty, staff and administrators, board members, and others can influence the environment the students experience at the institution. A college can enhance its programs, offer new opportunities, and otherwise shape the E that ultimately contributes to student outcomes. Because E is the key variable in Astin's equation, we will focus on it throughout the book. No matter the external constraints, from performance metrics and funding to student demographics and technological changes, all institutions have the capacity to create environments where students can learn and succeed.

Claims like that might cause you to wonder if the authors of this book are naively hopeful. Admittedly we are profoundly optimistic about the potential within colleges and universities. Yet we do know that resources and time are scarce, campus climates are less than ideal, and change is never easy. We are emphasizing possibilities not because we are wearing rose-colored glasses but rather because we have seen countless examples across the country of institutional and programmatic excellence. Often this quality is not widely acknowledged because it happens on campuses without high profiles or large endowments. And sometimes all of us are too busy doing the work to take the time to tell others about it. Yet these stories have a great deal to teach us about what is possible—and what is necessary.

Our world faces profound challenges in the years ahead: Social and environmental upheaval, economic inequality and stagnation, cultural and religious conflict, racial and ethnic oppression, personal and communal violence, and more. Not only do our students need and deserve high-quality educations, but our world also needs more people with the knowledge, skills, capacities, and commitments to make positive differences in their professions and communities. Higher education is one of the fundamental levers necessary to create a more sustainable, just, and humane future. Indeed, the mission of higher education is so important that we must act to make sure that we are successful in delivering what matters most in a student's education—and our actions must be guided by our values and aspirations, not short-term expediency or passing fads.

Using This Book

We have deliberately written a relatively brief and, we hope, engaging book that is relevant and accessible for a wide range of readers—from faculty, staff, and administrators to trustees, policymakers, philanthropists, alumni, parents, and students.

Our analysis throughout the book is based on our reading of the literature and our deep and diverse experiences in higher education. We aim to translate what we have seen in the scholarship and on the ground into an accessible and practical book. Too often, we believe, excellent higher education research does not yield the institutional change that it could because disciplinary conventions keep it from reaching a broad audience. At the same time, individual college or university success stories are dismissed because they are too idiosyncratic. By synthesizing the best scholarship and practice, and complementing that with insights gained throughout our careers, we hope to provide a useful framework and practical advice for a wide range of people who are interested in higher education.

The book aims to help you articulate and enact a concrete, aspirational vision for undergraduate education that will have a positive impact on your students, your institutions, and our world. To do that, each chapter explores one of the six core themes outlined earlier. The chapters begin with brief vignettes that illustrate the central issues, then analyze important action principles, and close with questions for reflection and discussion.

We suggest you approach the book from your own perspective, considering how the principles and practices we address connect to your work and role at your institution. Presidents and members of governing boards may focus more on large strategic questions; faculty and student affairs staff may think more about day-to-day interactions with students and colleagues. People in service roles on campus may reflect on the potential for their work to enhance the students' environment and educational mission of the institution. We urge you to think critically and creatively about how the ideas and examples in this book connect to, and challenge, your current practices. We hope the myriad examples will offer you visions of the possible, even though the particulars of a case might differ from yours.

Although you might be reading today on your own, we hope groups and institutions will use the book as a catalyst for discussions about what matters most for undergraduate education in your particular context. The questions at the end of each chapter may be useful prompts for deliberations about policies and practices within a department, school, or institution.

The future of undergraduate education will hinge on the questions that you ask and the decisions you make to act on what matters most. To thrive in the future, institutional leaders at all levels will need to question assumptions, critically inquire into the effectiveness of their work, and inventively approach new and persistent problems: Do you have a guiding vision to shape your work, and how do you systematically yet creatively enact that vision? What is the impact of the education you offer your students, and how can you enhance that impact for all of your students? What is the real value of an undergraduate education, not only to an individual but also to our communities and to our world?

We believe that questions like these need to guide all of our work in higher education. The coming chapters will explore what is possible when they do.

2

LEARNING MATTERS

Professor Paul Fessler thought he had seen it all in his many years on the faculty, but he had never experienced something like what happened in his class one fall day.

Fessler, a historian at Dordt College in Iowa, recently had made a big change in his teaching. He transformed his lecture-heavy Western Civilization course into a series of elaborate Reacting to the Past games, a pedagogy developed by Mark Carnes. Reacting to the Past immerses students in the intellectual and moral dilemmas of specific moments in history. For Fessler's class, students read texts by Jean-Jacques Rousseau, Edmund Burke, and other influential eighteenth-century thinkers before assuming roles as key figures in the French Revolution. In class, students debated royal power and human rights, each student arguing and writing from the perspective of an individual who was involved in the Revolution. Fessler thrilled at how seriously the students took on their roles and engaged with the ideas at hand, but now he faced an unusual request. Students petitioned Fessler to begin his morning class 30 minutes earlier each day, providing them more time to discuss the serious matters of the Revolution. He consented, and for the remainder of the semester, class began at 7:30 a.m.

Mark Carnes relates this story, and many more like it, in his book *Minds on Fire* (2014). According to Carnes, pedagogies like Reacting to the Past are antidotes to the student disengagement and drift portrayed in influential books including *Our Underachieving Colleges* (Bok, 2006), *Academically Adrift* (Arum & Roksa, 2011), and *Excellent Sheep* (Deresiewicz, 2014). The authors of these books argue that, even at the most selective institutions, students are meandering through college, learning little that lasts. Arum and Roksa (2011), for instance, report that students at a range of institutions share a similar, and distressing, definition of academic engagement: "the mere acts of showing up in class and turning in assignments" (p. 36). If students put in minimal effort and institutions focus resources and attention elsewhere, former Harvard president Derek Bok concludes, no one should be surprised that many students graduate with only limited and superficial learning.

Fessler and Carnes, however, demonstrate that the status quo is not inevitable. Indeed, Reacting to the Past, which Carnes pioneered at Barnard College in the 1990s, has yielded impressive outcomes with diverse students at all kinds of institutions. Many other pedagogical approaches, from peer instruction in introductory science, technology, engineering, and mathematics (STEM) courses (Drane, Micari, & Light, 2014) to well-designed writing assignments in any class (Anderson, Anson, Gonyea, & Paine, 2015) have been shown to produce significant student learning among undergraduates across the full spectrum of higher education institutions.

Research on learning in college continues to evolve, but we now know quite a lot about what most contributes to positive student learning outcomes. This research suggests that certain practices not only yield significant learning with traditional college students but also are even more effective with students who historically have been underserved on college campuses (Finley & McNair, 2013). No simple prescriptions or magic bullets exist, but we know more than ever before about how pedagogies, experiences, and curricular pathways contribute to learning. In other words, despite the diversity of both students and higher education institutions, evidence is increasingly clear about the common characteristics of effective undergraduate education. Our central challenge is to put these good practices into effect so that all of our students have the best possible opportunities to learn in college.

Learning Matters: Action Principles

1. Take institutional responsibility for student learning.
2. Create opportunities for learning in and out of the classroom.
3. Recognize the complexity of meaningful learning.
4. Help students integrate learning experiences.
5. Promote and reward learning for everyone at the institution.

Take Institutional Responsibility for Student Learning

Student learning is a primary goal of higher education, but sometimes it may seem that a college or university's success at meeting this goal is beyond its control. Students are responsible for their own learning—faculty and staff cannot learn for them.

If students fail to do the things they need to do to learn, that is largely their fault. Institutions are off the hook.

However, although student effort is crucial to their learning in college, institutions can play an essential role by influencing the shape and scope of the effort students make (American College Personnel Association, 1994; Wolf-Wendel, Ward, & Kinzie, 2009). Institutions create the environment for learning. The qualities of that environment go a long way to stimulate and scaffold, or to hinder and distract, students in the fundamental work of learning. And as Arum and Roksa (2011) explain, many students are not learning much in college because too often they are not being challenged to study hard. They drift because they can. Although institutions cannot learn for students, colleges and universities are responsible for building and sustaining environments that challenge and support all students to learn. As the Nobel Laureate and polymath Herbert A. Simon explained,

> Learning results from what the student does and thinks and only from what the student does and thinks. The teacher [and the college] can advance learning only by influencing what the student does to learn. (quoted in Ambrose, Bridges, DiPietro, Lovett, & Norman, 2010, p. 1)

Scholars have documented how a range of pedagogies, from lecturing to problem-based learning, prompts students to learn (Buskist & Groccia, 2012). Research from the National Survey of Student Engagement (NSSE) has established that certain practices are especially high impact (Kuh, 2008) for all students and have particularly positive outcomes for students who have traditionally been underserved in American higher education (Finley & McNair, 2013).

High-Impact Practices

First-year seminars and experiences	Learning communities
Common intellectual experiences	Writing-intensive courses
Collaborative assignments and projects	Undergraduate research
Service-learning/community-based learning	Diversity/global learning
Capstone courses and projects	Internships

Source: Kuh (2008).

Although Kuh's (2008) high-impact practices have garnered a great deal of attention, neither this list nor the other rich research on effective pedagogies has produced a revolution in the undergraduate experience. NSSE results, for instance, reveal only a modest increase in the number of students participating in high-impact practices from 2006 to 2012, and the proportion of first-generation students engaging in these practices continues to lag behind the rates for undergraduates who have college-educated parents (Finley & McNair, 2013, p. 8).

The slow pace of change reveals in part the difficulty of implementing some of these practices in all undergraduate settings; study abroad, for instance, may be financially and practically impossible for some students, such as a working single parent attending a community college or a low-income student who must support himself with a job throughout his college years. Despite obstacles like this, all institutions can enhance student learning by focusing more on the qualities that make *any* experience or pedagogy high impact rather than concentrating solely on a circumscribed list of practices. Indeed, research demonstrates that quality matters; even Kuh's 10 high-impact practices must be done well for students to learn from them (McNair & Albertine, 2012). Service-learning, internships, and other community-based experiences, for instance, are likely to yield student learning only when structured and facilitated effectively (Eyler, 2009). As John Dewey (1910) noted long ago, experience alone is not sufficient for meaningful learning to result; the context of and reflection on experience are essential factors, too.

In 1987, Arthur Chickering and Zelda Gamson outlined seven principles for good practice in undergraduate education:

1. It encourages contact between students and faculty.

2. It develops reciprocity and cooperation among students.

3. It encourages active learning.

4. It gives prompt feedback.

5. It emphasizes time on task.

6. It communicates high expectations.

7. It respects diverse talents and ways of learning.

These principles remain the basis for most measures of quality today. For instance, Kuh and O'Donnell (2013, p. 10) drew from them when they sketched the essential elements of any high-impact practice:

1. Performance expectations set at appropriately high levels

2. Significant investment of time and effort by students over an extended period of time

3. Interactions with faculty and peers about substantive matters

4. Experiences with diversity, wherein students are exposed to and must contend with people and circumstances that differ from those with which students are familiar

5. Frequent, timely, and constructive feedback

6. Periodic, structured opportunities to reflect and integrate learning

7. Opportunities to discover relevance of learning through real-world applications

8. Public demonstration of competence

In short, all high-impact pedagogies or experiences should prompt students to engage in challenging work, interact with peers and mentors in meaningful ways, and reflect on what is being learned. When these elements are prioritized in the design and implementation of an educational activity, they allow many experiences in and out of the classroom to have positive impacts on student learning.

Mount Holyoke College in Massachusetts aimed to do precisely this in a major initiative called Making the Lynk. Faculty at Mount Holyoke were troubled by the difficulty many students seemed to have connecting their liberal arts education with their plans for work and life after graduation. The college could not make that link for students, nor could it fill this gap with a single high-impact practice. However, it could more effectively facilitate student reflection and meaning making about their studies and future. Drawing on research about integrative learning and high-impact practices, faculty worked together through a planning process that "imagined curriculum-to-career as something that was not just an add-on that was delivered beyond the faculty—parallel to the regular curriculum—or in one specialized program serving a few students. The vision, as it developed, was an ambitious plan to embed the resources of career preparation directly into the liberal arts core for every student" (Townsley, Packard, & Paus, 2015, p. 26).

In 2013, Mount Holyoke began to implement Making the Lynk across campus. For academic departments, this involved a multiyear process of curricular and pedagogical change, supported by significant institutional resources, to help students do the intellectual work of connecting their liberal arts courses with experiential learning opportunities on and off campus. Departments and faculty collaborated with colleagues in the career center, academic advising, the internship office, college communications, and other areas to ensure that "the curriculum-to-career idea is embedded strategically: in assessment initiatives, communication plans, staffing and infrastructure decisions, alumnae relations, and ongoing curricular development" (Townsley et al., 2015, p. 29).

In a similar way, student life staff at the University of Iowa applied the elements of high-impact practices to transform the learning of the more than 2,000 students employed in the division's jobs each semester. Staff developed a program called Iowa GROW (Guided Reflection on Work) that prompts student workers to regularly reflect on and integrate their workplace learning with their academic studies and their future plans. At least twice each semester, a supervisor and a student worker meet for a brief conversation framed around a few simple questions:

1. How is this job fitting in with your academics?

2. What are you learning here at work that is helping you in school?

3. What are you learning in class that you can apply here at work?

4. Can you give me a couple of examples of things that you are learning here at work that you will be using in your future profession? (Vice President for Student Life, n.d.)

The results of this brief but repeated intervention are striking. GROW students are more likely than other student workers on Iowa's campus to report that their jobs helped them improve their writing, speaking, and time-management skills and that the jobs also challenged them to interact with people from different backgrounds and cultures (Gose, 2014). Since other research (Pascarella & Terenzini, 2005) reveals that on-campus work is a more positive predictor of degree attainment than working off campus, programs like Iowa GROW hold the potential to contribute to both individual student learning and also broader institutional goals.

Institutional efforts to enhance student outcomes often become expensive and unwieldy. Not only does GROW illustrate the power of simple reflective practices, but it also underscores how small interventions can have significant outcomes on the undergraduate experience. Although large-scale change sometimes is required, more targeted steps often are most effective. Daniel Chambliss and Christopher Takacs (2014) emphasize in their study of learning at Hamilton College that "there are methods—simultaneously reliable, powerful, available, and cheap—for improving what students gain from college. Such methods consistently work well, handsomely repay whatever effort goes into them, can be used by almost anyone, and require not much time and almost no additional money" (p. 1).

A 2014 NSSE report comes to a similar conclusion about the possibility of low-cost, focused interventions: "Institutions with lower selectivity profiles can and often do offer experiences with faculty that are at least comparable to those at more selective institutions" (National Survey of Student Engagement, 2014, p. 11). The research is clear: Systematic small steps by faculty, staff, and institutions can yield big gains for student learning.

Create Opportunities for Learning in and out of the Classroom

In his classic study of student learning at Harvard, Richard Light (2001) highlights a surprising finding: "I assumed the most important and memorable academic learning goes on inside the classroom, while outside activities provide a useful but modest supplement. The evidence shows the opposite is true ... When we asked students to think of a specific, critical incident or moment that had changed them profoundly, four-fifths of them chose a situation or event outside the classroom" (p. 8).

The curriculum clearly is essential to the undergraduate experience, but too often colleges are reluctant to recognize and validate the important learning that takes place beyond the classroom. Ken O'Donnell (2013) notes that a study he conducted with colleagues in the Office of the Chancellor of the California State University echoed what Light reports: "HIPs (high-impact practices) survive on the margins, like opportunistic mammals in the Jurassic Age, tolerated only so long as they don't get in the way of the dinosaurs" (p. 16). A pair of national surveys confirmed that not only are these high-impact practices frequently viewed as less significant than what takes place in the classroom but also that only a fraction of the undergraduate population typically is able to participate in them on most campuses (Barefoot, Griffin, & Koch, 2012; Koch, Griffin, & Barefoot, 2014).

Despite the challenges of enacting high-impact experiences in and out of the classroom, O'Donnell (2013) argues that "bringing [these effective practices] to scale doesn't mean inventing them from scratch, or even convincing our colleagues of their merit; we're well beyond that. Instead, it means making them visible, credit-bearing, and funded, so they can count toward our degrees. It means making them legitimate" (p. 16).

Indeed, the surveys cited in the previous paragraph found that even chronically underresourced community colleges have created fertile soil for high-impact pedagogies and practices to grow; for instance, 55% of community colleges offer academic service-learning courses, and 23% support undergraduate research (Koch et al., 2014). And, of course, every institution has rigorous and effective faculty who challenge students to learn more than they thought possible. When these faculty teach with active learning pedagogies, even in the largest lecture courses, students can learn and succeed (Freeman, Eddy, McDonough, Smith, Okoroafor, Jordt, & Wenderoth, 2014).

This suggests that institutions have existing assets and models of excellence on which to build. The problem is the disjuncture between where learning actually happens and the way higher education traditionally accounts for learning through course credits, seat time, and such. To resolve this conflict, institutions must move the most effective learning practices from the margins to the center of the student experience, which often requires expanding conceptions of where learning can and does happen in higher education.

The California State University System is aiming to do just that through its Give Students a Compass project, part of a broader initiative from the Association of American Colleges and Universities (AAC&U) involving public institutions in three states. For the California State system, Compass strives to integrate high-impact practices into the state's general education transfer curriculum, ensuring that an increasing number of students across the system engage in more of these powerful educational experiences. For instance, a partnership between faculty at Cosumnes River College (CRC), a community college, and nearby Sacramento State University, to where many CRC students transfer, created faculty learning communities that worked together to link the pedagogies and outcomes of general education courses that spanned the two institutions and established an electronic portfolio (e-portfolio) platform that students could use at both institutions to reflect on and document their learning. Through a large number of similar partnerships, Compass quickly reached thousands of students across the state, providing a more engaging first two years of college and a more intellectually coherent transfer experience in general education and also improving graduation and retention rates (David, 2013).

Such initiatives have proved particularly effective with traditionally underserved students. For instance, the University of Michigan created the Undergraduate Research Opportunity Program (UROP) to directly connect students with the research mission of the university without changing the curriculum or courses. The program invites first- and second-year undergraduates to work with faculty across campus on academic projects. Peer mentors facilitate noncredit seminars to help UROP participants link their individual research projects with broader themes in their disciplines and across the university. Despite being entirely outside the curriculum, UROP contributes to many positive student outcomes, including increased retention, academic performance, and pursuit of postgraduate education, with the greatest benefits accruing to Black males (University of Michigan, 2015).

To tackle the lower retention and graduation rates of junior transfers from community colleges, the University of North Carolina at Chapel Hill launched the Transfer United (TU) living-learning initiative. Bringing together staff and faculty from across campus, the TU program connects students with learning opportunities and resources from academic affairs, residence life, community service, peer tutoring, and the career center. In the program's required seminar course, TU students conduct autoethnography research projects focused on their own transitions to the university. Through weekly field work, including interviews and observations on campus, TU students learn about their new community while reflecting on their own successes and struggles in their first semester (Fink & Hummel, 2015). With TU, transfer students are immersed in the many educational resources of the university, empowering them to take fuller advantage of all the institution has to offer both in and out of the classroom. Assessment results from the first cohorts of Transfer United demonstrate both a high retention rate (more than 95% one-year retention) and that participating students feel supported within the university community (Fisher, Demetriou, & Hall, 2013).

In all three of these examples, institutions have made an often peripheral aspect of the student experience, such as general education or noncredit research, a central facet of undergraduate learning.

Recognize the Complexity of Meaningful Learning

While working to learn something, people often struggle, and sometimes they fail. Misunderstandings, misconceptions, and outright mistakes line the path to enlightenment. As Martin Covington (1992) explains, "Failure is interesting partly for the fact that successful thinkers actually make more mistakes than those who give up easily and therefore preserve their unblemished record of mediocrity, and also for the fact that mistakes can usually be set right by trying again" (p. 231).

If only the successful outcomes of learning are measured and rewarded, learners may not see the value in stretching themselves. To develop students (and faculty, staff, and administrators) who have the habits and capacities necessary to learn in the face of challenges, institutions must recognize and value the complexity of learning. This principle has implications for the ways students (and others) are evaluated, of course, but it also requires institutions to create incentives for all learners to accept and to value struggles and failures on the way toward positive change.

Constructive alignment is a practical framework for designing the supports and rewards necessary for complex learning (Biggs & Tang, 2011). In educational environments from classrooms to internship sites and campus offices, misalignments often exist among the goals, the learning processes, and the outcomes. For instance, a faculty member teaching an intermediate-level Spanish language course may set as a goal that her students become capable and confident writers of academic essays in Spanish. She may design varied activities to give students writing practice. However, if she deducts multiple points for every grammatical and conjugation error on each writing task, students may adopt strategies to preserve their grades like using only simple, familiar words and phrases in all of their compositions. Even though the faculty member might become frustrated that her students are not stretching themselves, the heart of the problem is that her grading practices do not align with her goals. If the faculty member wants students to push themselves as writers, she needs to create incentives for them to stretch, which might mean sometimes lessening the penalties for mechanical errors and rewarding students for taking intellectual or compositional risks.

A simple approach toward this end, according to Therese Huston (2009, p. 196), is "to normalize help-seeking behaviors." Undergraduates are often uncomfortable revealing their confusion about course material. This can be particularly acute for students who have doubts about whether they belong in college or in a discipline, such as first-generation students or females in male-dominated disciplines. In such situations, students often feel intense performance anxiety (Steele, 1997, 2010). To help students overcome such concerns, course policies like requiring a brief face-to-face meeting with the faculty member or teaching assistant in the first few weeks of the term can have powerful effects by beginning to establish a relationship that will be important as the course unfolds. In online courses, a similar goal can be achieved by creating a welcome forum in the learning management system "where students get to know one another [and the faculty member] in a low-stakes, casual environment before jumping into the more challenging assignments" (Miller, 2014, p. 146). Such approaches have positive outcomes for students, but they can be equally effective for faculty and staff. As John Tagg (2003) notes, a learning organization values constructive failures and encourages individuals to acknowledge the limits of understanding.

Northern Arizona University's First-Year Learning Initiative (FYLI) offers a comprehensive approach toward recognizing and valuing the complexity of learning. FYLI focuses on effective design in foundational courses that are taken by large numbers of first- and second-year students at Northern Arizona, the kinds of classes that historically have served as gateways to academic majors and that often have relatively high rates of failure and withdrawal. FYLI aims not only to teach students important course content but also to develop in students the skills and attitudes they will need to be successful in college. All FYLI courses, for instance, take a small-bites approach to assessment, providing students with frequent feedback on their performance, often through online tools. FYLI courses also make a rich array of learning resources available to students online, including rubrics for all graded work and extensive bridging activities that help students practice disciplinary techniques and compare their own work with models from experts. FYLI relies heavily on instructional technology, and some courses in the program are hybrid or fully online; yet the guiding philosophy of the initiative is consistent regardless of the course format. And all FYLI courses have peer teaching assistants who give students support with and feedback on their work and also strive to make asking for help a routine part of being a new undergraduate at Northern Arizona. Research on both student behaviors in FYLI and course completion rates demonstrate the effectiveness of this systematic approach to the complex tasks students face early in their undergraduate careers (Miller, 2014).

Broad approaches like FYLI work well, but technological change increasingly is making even more personally responsive education possible. George Siemens argues that "we're moving from a model where we forced one teaching method on hundreds of students in a class to a model where we can personalize the education of every student on campus" (quoted in Selingo, 2013, p. 74). By combining research from the learning sciences with data analysis from thousands of students taking technology-enabled courses, projects like the Open Learning Initiative at Carnegie Mellon University are creating online courses that automatically adapt to an individual student's performance through intelligent tutoring systems that provide personalized feedback and hints as students struggle to master course content and skills (Koedinger Kim, Jia, McLaughlin, & Bier, 2015). These courses acknowledge the complexity of learning and create environments where learners are motivated to work hard by completing, often after several failed attempts, progressively more challenging tasks (Gee, 2003).

This cycle of failure and success that students experience in this kind of situated learning need not be limited to online environments, of course. Reacting to the Past, profiled at the beginning of this chapter, offers a different, face-to-face model toward the same end. As Mark Carnes (2014), the pioneer of Reacting, notes, "Well-intentioned teachers, seeking to create positive classroom experiences, often err in creating activities with little or no risk of failure" (p. 175). Carnes maintains that students need to be invited and challenged to engage intellectually and emotionally with the ideas and skills they are learning in college. Learning, after all, is as complex as students are.

Help Students Integrate Learning Experiences

Undergraduate learning must be more than simply adding up discrete credits until the total equals the number necessary for a credential. Institutional mission statements, and our students' aspirations, aim much higher than that. We promise that our graduates will be able to integrate and synthesize their learning from the curriculum and other experiences, allowing them to transfer what they have learned into new settings within and beyond the campus. Indeed, the ability to connect disparate information and make meaning in dynamic situations is widely considered to be essential for success in the modern economy (Barber, 2012). In a nutshell, "most fundamentally, our educational mission is to prepare students to understand and contribute to a world that is increasingly complex and interconnected" (Newman, Carpenter, Grawe, & Jaret-McKinstry, 2015, p. 14).

Unfortunately, research suggests that many students are not as successful as they could or should be at integrating and transferring their learning from one context to another (Arum & Roksa, 2011; Nowacek, 2011; Wardle, 2007). For students to develop these capacities, they need multiple opportunities to practice doing so in courses, in the co-curriculum, and in off-campus experiences. Too often, that simply does not happen. Richard Keeling and Richard Hersh (2012) contend that the fundamental problem is that learning "is fractured on our campuses ... divided not by bad intentions, but by traditions, tensions, and training" (p. 64). If institutions cannot span disciplinary and organizational boundaries, how can we expect students to integrate their learning experiences into a coherent whole?

Carleton College, a liberal arts institution in Minnesota, has been working for years to cultivate integrative learning. Carleton faculty have developed three intersecting curricular projects that focus on transfer and synthesis across the disciplines. Visualizing the Liberal Arts emphasizes the importance of visual images, media, and models as tools for making meaning in the world. Quantitative Inquiry, Reasoning, and Knowledge focuses on the use, analysis, application, and communication of quantitative evidence in all fields of study. The Global Engagement Initiative concentrates on thinking across boundaries by integrating language study, courses in diverse disciplines, off-campus study, internships, and civic engagement opportunities. While these three initiatives began separately, as they developed, the Carleton faculty came to recognize that integrative learning requires integrative teaching, so they increasingly have found ways to connect these initiatives and to identify other opportunities to prompt students to bring together learning in and out of the classroom. Summarizing nearly a decade's worth of work, the leaders of these initiatives conclude, "At Carleton, integrative learning thrives when faculty and staff working collaboratively and with strong administrative support see themselves as collectively responsible for the learning of their students in ways that transcend specific courses, departments, or programs" (Newman et al., 2015, p. 15).

As the Carleton example suggests, one powerful strategy to enhance integrative learning is to make course and program planning efforts collaborative. Based on years of study of faculty and institutions across the country, Dee Fink (2013) contends that course design is perhaps the single most important activity faculty engage in to improve student learning. Although faculty customarily create their syllabi on their own, a growing number of institutions are hosting initiatives that invite faculty to work with peers, other campus professionals, or even students to redesign courses (Cook-Sather, Bovill, & Felten, 2014; Palmer, Bach, & Streifer, 2014). For instance, Dan Bernstein and Andrea Greenhoot, psychology faculty at the University of Kansas, teamed with librarians and writing center staff to improve a gateway course in their major. After analyzing the results of their own experience and that of a number of similar projects at Kansas, they concluded that "designing a course collaboratively with a team of specialists is both a valuable and viable instructional innovation. Gathering the skills of many people is a very good way (and maybe the only way) to meet the challenge of large-enrollment lower-division courses" (quoted in Bailey, Jaggars, & Jenkins, 2015, p. 103). Indeed, any complex program in higher education, in or outside the classroom, could benefit from a diverse design team working together to create meaningful learning experiences for students.

The online baccalaureate nursing (BSN) program at Arizona State University illustrates the power of collaboration across academic departments. As in many nursing programs, faculty at Arizona State identified writing as an essential skill for graduates—and as one that undergraduates in this program did not systematically learn in the curriculum. To change this, nursing faculty partnered with faculty from the university's technical communication program to develop and implement a new online course that built on the disciplinary expertise of the writing faculty and the learning goals of the nursing faculty. This writing course immerses students in scenarios requiring them to research and write a series of documents for different readers: "Through sequencing assignments, students grasp a more sophisticated understanding of writing in the workplace, including the methods to understand the purpose of their writing and the audience to whom it will be directed" (Stevens, D'Angelo, Rennell, Muzyka, Pannabecker, & Maid, 2014, p. 19). The outcomes of this course, now in its third year, are positive, although challenges of collaboration remain including the need to hire or support nursing faculty who are well prepared to teach writing within their discipline.

Ohio University's Designing to Make a Difference (DMAD) capstone experience in mechanical engineering illustrates the potential of both collaborative planning and integrative learning. DMAD evolved over a decade of faculty-led efforts to create project-based learning that meets the aspirations of the department, the goals of students who will soon be joining the profession, the requirements of accreditors, and the needs of the university's community in Appalachia. DMAD connects across the curriculum through weekly interactions between first-year undergraduates taking Introduction to Mechanical Engineering and seniors in the capstone; the new students see how engineering can meet real community needs, and the seniors develop their professional skills with presentations and mentoring activities. DMAD seniors engage with alumni and others in the region in order to receive feedback on their design plans from mechanical engineers who are not on the faculty. By integrating disciplinary learning with professional development, DMAD produces powerful outcomes for students including both high employment rates for graduates and the cultivation of capacities that will help alumni succeed throughout their careers. One student, for example, reflected:

My personal skill development project through the year was to try to do things that maybe I'm not good at already so that I can learn to do these things. I will have to do this once I have a job so avoiding projects that are uncomfortable for me now won't help me NOT avoid them when I'm a part of the work force. I improved this quarter by taking up more of the design report than I did in the past. I wrote the whole section instead of just helping with a few sections. I gained a sense of confidence in my own work. There was a lot riding on the work I was doing because it affects my whole team. (Quoted in Kremer, 2013, p. 49)

This kind of deep, integrative learning is most possible when individuals and institutions are willing to bridge disciplinary and other traditional boundaries to make student learning the central priority of their work.

Promote and Reward Learning for Everyone at the Institution

To meet evolving student needs, to implement practices informed by emerging research, and to remain agile in a changing higher education environment, institutions and individuals must themselves continue to learn. John Tagg (2003) calls this the golden rule for higher education: "Do what you want your students to do. Be what you want your students to be" (p. 347). Like the original, the simplicity of this version of the rule is its strength. Everyone in an institution can apply the rule personally, and it can be applied to the college itself. The rule also sets an aspirational vision, aligning our own actions with the goals and hopes we have for our students.

As with student learning, mindsets shape possibilities for faculty and staff development. Research by O'Meara, Terosky, and Neumann (2008) uncovered widespread beliefs held in higher education that most faculty are so busy "'just making it,' 'treading water,' 'dodging bullets,' or barely 'staying alive'" that they resist change (p. 20). These authors label this a "narrative of constraint" that, although both real and important, obscures the possibility of "faculty's professional growth even amid scarcity, turbulence, and ambiguity" (p. 3). A "narrative of growth", on the other hand, frames faculty as having "the desire and will to craft themselves as teachers, researchers, and partners in service and community engagement who have actively chosen—and continue actively to choose—the academic career as a way to lead their lives" (p. 19). These narratives, either implicitly or explicitly, shape both the practices and the funding of faculty development on many campuses. An institution operating within a narrative of constraint considers faculty development to be something done to hostile or disengaged faculty; requirements and a check-box mentality often rule the day. A narrative of growth, on the other hand, leads to faculty development initiatives emerging from the professional goals and habits of a busy faculty who willingly seek the expertise and perspectives of peers.

LaGuardia Community College, of the City University of New York, is a model of what is possible when faculty development occurs within a narrative of growth. For more than a decade, the LaGuardia faculty has worked with strong administrative support to construct an "inquiry-based outcomes assessment process that supports institutional learning, advances faculty's reflective professional practice, and most importantly, improves student learning" (Arcario, Eynon, Klages, & Polnariev, 2013, p. 21). LaGuardia faculty developed this process by first articulating a shared set of general education student competencies that stretch across the curriculum and then implementing a robust e-portfolio system where students capture and reflect on evidence of their learning related to these competencies. LaGuardia's Center for Teaching and Learning (CTL) not only supports faculty in integrating the e-portfolio work into their classes but also helps faculty develop rubrics to evaluate each of the competencies. Teams of faculty then score representative evidence from e-portfolios to assess student performance at different points in the curriculum. When faculty in the business administration and business management programs were disappointed by their students' performances on oral competency assessments, they used a grant from the CTL to partner with faculty from communication studies to revise the oral communication assignments used in many introductory business courses. After a review of the evidence from e-portfolios demonstrated the efficacy of these changes, the faculty decided to adopt them in all introductory courses and also to better scaffold oral communication skills in other classes in the program (Arcario et al., 2013, p. 31).

The willingness of LaGuardia faculty to seek out and to respond to student underperformance, even failure, is essential for positive institutional change. Too often, just as faculty development occurs within a narrative of constraint, assessment initiatives operate within a "culture of compliance" (Ikenberry & Kuh, 2015, p. 5) that values reporting over authentic inquiry. Failures are elided in favor of bromides that create the illusion of performance. This negative orientation not only harms individual students but also weakens institutions and higher education as a whole. Colleges and universities can no longer afford to deny bad news and resist evidence-informed reforms. Pat Hutchings, Mary Huber, and Tony Ciccone (2011) neatly capture the situation: "Educational innovation today invites, even requires, levels of preparation, imagination, collaboration, and support that are not always a good fit (to say the least) with the inherited routines of academic life" (p. 6).

Conclusion

Learning is a fundamental purpose of any college or university. To live into that goal, institutions must make the paradigm shift that Barr and Tagg (1995) called for two decades ago—from teaching to learning. This is a devilishly difficult task because so many of our policies and practices continue to be rooted in what Barr and Tagg call the instructional paradigm: We organize our institutions around credit hours and course loads, equating learning with seat time. Although the learning paradigm has been widely embraced since Barr and Tagg coined the term, the instructional paradigm remains the practice on most campuses.

Still, narratives change. Just as we work to help our students become more engaged and resilient learners, we must cultivate our colleagues and institutions as learners with the potential to grow and thrive. This may require significant changes for individuals and organizations as we transform into learning-centered institutions. Goals and evaluation policies must be aligned, both in practice and in perception, so that our students and our colleagues understand that we really mean it when we say that learning matters most.

Questions for Reflection

1. What is your role in student learning at your institution? How do you, and your institution, measure your effectiveness? What areas for improvement do you see in your efforts? What can you do to be more effective?

2. What pedagogies or programs at your institution create engaging and integrated learning? How can you make these programs even more effective? How can you make these programs available to more students?

3. How do you currently, or how might you, use the essential elements of high-impact practices to develop powerful

learning experiences for students both in and outside the classroom?

4. Where is integrative learning most likely to occur at your campus? What could you do to support more integrative learning for students, faculty, and staff?

5. How does your institution, and how do you, respond to struggle and failure? What can you do to create a climate where failure can be a step toward learning? What actions can you take to incorporate this way of thinking into your own work and into programs and systems at your institution?

6. How is learning promoted and rewarded for faculty and staff at your institution? What are some creative new ways that learning could be supported?

7. What can you do to learn more and to contribute more to your peers' learning?

3

RELATIONSHIPS MATTER

I n the world of elite higher education, what makes the Duke undergraduate experience distinct? According to Stephen Nowicki and Lee D. Baker, two top administrators at the university, the Duke difference is the intentional focus on programs to foster meaningful relationships between undergraduates and faculty within a research university environment. The institution connects three signature initiatives—undergraduate research, civic and global engagement, and interdisciplinary learning—to help students build knowledge across disciplines and develop relationships with peers and faculty mentors.

To ensure these relationships are powerful, Duke begins with admissions. The university deliberately admits a diverse student body, drawing from around the country and across the globe. Multiple studies demonstrate that students who interact frequently with racially and ethnically diverse peers show greater growth in intellectual engagement than those who do not (e.g., Chang, Denson, Saenz, & Misa, 2006; Gurin, Nagda, & Lopez, 2004; Pascarella & Terenzini, 2005). Extending this research into other aspects of identity, Duke strives for an "an authentic integration of values, ideas, religions, cultures, and politics" and hopes that relationship building across difference will help students learn to develop empathy for others and to disagree civilly, essential tools for an institutional mission aligned with a commitment to civic engagement (Nowicki & Baker, 2015).

Representational diversity, however, does not guarantee relationships will flourish across difference, so Duke encourages first-year students to participate in the Focus program, which enrolls students in two classes of a three- or four-class cluster organized around themes such as cognitive neuroscience and law; ethics, leadership, and global citizenship; or epigenetics, environmental genomics, and ethics. Focus students also enroll in a weekly discussion seminar in which all cluster faculty and students participate. And cluster students are housed in the same residence hall to foster out-of-classroom dialogue and interaction, including university-sponsored off-campus service and other experiential activities.

Nowicki and Baker emphasize that institutions must seed opportunities for relationship building. Two simple and replicable initiatives illustrate this approach. Duke's FLUNCH program funds opportunities for students to invite faculty members for one-on-one lunches. Baker reports that the number of times a faculty member has been FLUNCHed has become somewhat of a status symbol at Duke. In a similar vein, since assessment results indicate that students value opportunities to dine in faculty homes, Duke created the FINvite program to ease the logistical and preparatory burdens on faculty. Duke caters a simple dinner and provides transportation for students to free up faculty members to think about hosting intellectually engaging salons in their homes.

Duke administrators frankly acknowledge that the institution has underinvested in spaces for student engagement, particularly in student residences. Like many universities with established residence halls built for an earlier age, there are not enough common areas to encourage interaction. Administrators aim to develop new spaces that encourage Duke community members to "stick and sit" rather than "grab and go," such as an on-campus pub created at the initiative of the Student Government Undergraduate Intellectual Climate Committee (Spector, 2012) intended to be a place where students could have meaningful, casual conversations with peers and faculty on campus.

Because relationships are central to Duke's ambitions for undergraduates, Nowicki contends that administrators need to be "constantly on the lookout for grassroots efforts and then ask how we gently might support them" (Nowicki & Baker, 2015). Such attention has led to a recent initiative aimed at minimizing the technical and transactional details of academic advising relationships so that faculty can devote more of their time to addressing their students' questions and big picture goals. The Duke difference, after all, is building meaningful relationships.

Relationships Matter: Action Principles

1. Make relationships central to learning.
2. Create pathways to lead students into relationships with peers, faculty, and staff.
3. Nurture both learning and belonging through relationships.
4. Encourage everyone on campus to cultivate relationships.
5. Celebrate and reward relationship building.

Make Relationships Central to Learning

As we explained in Chapter 2, research on student learning in college has identified the characteristics that make certain educational experiences particularly high impact (Kuh, 2008). A central finding of this research is that high-impact practices are powerful in part because they are relationship rich (Brownell & Swaner, 2010).

Faculty–student, staff–student, and peer-to-peer relationships are at the very core of these practices. For instance,

Undergraduate research is a process that, at its best, moves students to new levels as learners and inquirers. The relationship between mentor and protégée can be transformative because it is rooted in an ongoing, substantive interaction around an essential part of the academic enterprise, scholarly research. Undergraduate research provides a strong foundation for diverse careers and graduate study, and a student's relationship with his or her mentor often persists long after graduation (Hensel, 2012).

Learning communities connect student learning in and out of the classroom by creating meaningful, boundary-spanning relationships. Whether through a relatively simple model of linked courses or in a more complex living–learning or residential college system, these programs immerse students in a community of peers, often supplemented by staff and faculty advisers, to challenge and support their academic and personal development. Classroom dialogues can more easily spill over into informal, out-of-class conversations when classmates live in close proximity to one another. With a relatively modest amount of planning, routine dining experiences can be transformed into powerful discussion sessions between faculty and students. Faculty and staff living in apartments within residence halls enjoy daily, informal interactions with students, giving undergraduates windows into the work and lives of busy professionals (Benjamin, 2015).

Senior capstone projects and courses provide an opportunity for integration and synthesis of a course of study, mentored by a faculty member, usually in the student's major. For instance, Professor Safia Swimelar's course for international relations majors at Elon requires students to complete major multimedia projects focused on geographic areas and expressed through poetry, music, novels, journalism, and blog posts and then to reflect on how aspects of globalization they have encountered affect local issues they experience in the United States. This course is rooted in relationships, as students work in small groups weekly and individually meet with Swimelar frequently to get feedback on both their research project and their reflective essays. Because of this personal engagement, a capstone "can be a transformative educational experience for students and faculty alike" (Hauhart & Grahe, 2015, p. 11).

Service-learning and related community-based pedagogies immerse students in contexts and relationships with off-campus partners and programs such as those involved with a neighborhood group working together with students in sociology and architecture courses to improve housing quality and affordability or a non-profit collaborating with landowners and environmental studies courses to restore a wetland. At their best, these experiences marry academic study with real community needs to produce powerful learning that connects theory to practice in a discipline. They also lead to civic outcomes including new understandings and capacities to navigate cultural differences and to analyze social systems. All of these depend on developing reciprocal, authentic relationships among students, faculty, and community partners (Felten & Clayton, 2011).

Although high-impact practices often reach outside the classroom, relationships are also key to learning in traditional courses. For example, Adam Rich cultivates peer-to-peer learning in his 170-student sophomore-level anatomy and physiology course at The College at Brockport: State University of New York. Rich uses simple technological tools to have his students respond to questions during his lectures. After students have submitted their initial answers, they talk in small groups and as a class about the reasons that certain responses are or are not correct. Students then submit second answers to the same question. Rich uses this real-time data about his students' comprehension to shape his lectures. He finds that students not only enjoy these sessions but more importantly also learn from their discussions about complex questions (Bruff, 2009). The research on such peer-to-peer pedagogies demonstrates that, compared with classes where students are not engaged with peers, "learning gains nearly triple" when "students are given the opportunity to resolve misunderstandings about concepts and work together to learn new ideas and skills in a discipline" (Mazur, 2009, p. 51).

Relationships are not only important for students. More than two decades ago, Lee Shulman (1993) lamented the "pedagogical solitude" of most faculty, claiming that "the reason teaching is not more valued in the academy is because the way we treat teaching removes it from the community of scholars"

(p. 6). Influential reform efforts have built on Shulman's insight, including the Science Education Initiatives (SEI) at the University of Colorado and the University of British Columbia. On both campuses, SEI work focuses on evidence-based change in teaching strategies in science and engineering courses. Unlike many reform projects that support individual faculty, SEI concentrates on academic departments. By fostering faculty peer-to-peer relationships around pedagogical change in a department, SEI has sparked a transformation in the teaching practices undergraduates experience in participating departments, reaching more than 75% of undergraduate credit hours taught in four science, technology, engineering, and mathematics (STEM) departments at Colorado and British Columbia in just three years. Faculty in these departments report that "being able to think about and discuss teaching with their colleagues as a serious scholarly activity" has been an important motivator for this change (Wieman, Perkins, & Gilbert, 2010, p. 13). Relationships are also essential to faculty learning.

Create Pathways to Lead Students into Relationships with Peers, Faculty, and Staff

A 2014 Gallup and Purdue University poll of 30,000 college graduates from across the United States studied the relationship between workplace engagement (a measure of "being intellectually and emotionally connected with their organizations and work teams because they are able to do what they do best, that they like what they do at work, and they have someone who cares about their development at work") and well-being ("such as finding fulfillment in daily work and interactions, having strong social relationships and access to resources people need, feeling financially secure, being physically healthy, and taking part in a true community").

The poll revealed that if students had a professor who (a) cared about them as individuals, (b) made them excited about learning, and (c) encouraged them to pursue their dreams, then—years later—their odds of being engaged at work more than doubled, as did their odds of reporting higher overall well-being. Unfortunately, only 14% of surveyed graduates experienced all three of these characteristics of a transformative student–faculty relationship while they were in college. Some fraction of that small number can be explained by serendipity—when the right people cross paths at the right time. Although these coincidences often yield remarkable results, higher education institutions should not leave relationship building to mere chance. The stakes are too high.

The poll further found that if these graduates had internships or jobs when they were still in college—where they were able to apply what they were learning in the classroom—were actively involved in extracurricular activities and organizations, and worked on projects that took a semester or more to complete, their odds of being engaged at work after college doubled. This finding supports the idea that high-impact learning practices also may have a postgraduation carryover effect.

The Gallup and Purdue University (2014) poll findings are in line with a large number of academic studies that have demonstrated the power of both formal and informal mentoring in higher education. W. Brad Johnson (2007) summarizes this research succinctly:

Good developmental relationships (mentorships)
promote socialization, learning, career advancement,
psychological adjustment, and preparation for
leadership. Compared to nonmentored individuals,
those with mentors tend to be more satisfied with their
careers, enjoy more promotions and higher income,
report greater commitment to the organization or
profession, and are more likely to mentor others in
turn. (p. 4)

Echoing Johnson's findings, Daniel F. Chambliss and
Christopher G. Takacs (2014) conclude their decade-long
study of students at Hamilton College in upstate New York
by arguing:

Relationships shape in detail students' experience: what
courses they take or majors they declare; whether they
play a sport or join an extracurricular activity; whether
they gain skills, grow ethically, or learn whatever is
offered in various programs. Relationships are important
because they raise or suppress the motivation to learn; a
good college fosters the relationships that lead to
motivation. (p. 155)

Chambliss and Takacs (2014) use the metaphor of pathways to explain how institutions guide students through their undergraduate years, from admissions through graduation (and beyond). Colleges carefully construct certain pathways for students such as a core curriculum (at Hamilton, an open one), academic majors, and formal convocations and other campus ceremonies. Whether the college wants them to be or not, other pathways like how to find parties on weekends also are brightly lit for students. On many campuses, however, no pathways are apparent for essential parts of the undergraduate experience. Are new students told how habits formed the first months of college often persist? Do institutions set an expectation for students to form at least one new important relationship with a mentor each term? Could colleges and universities take steps to facilitate simple and inexpensive programmatic opportunities to get students and faculty to sit down and talk, like FLUNCH at Duke? Chambliss and Takacs make it clear that institutions should take responsibility for creating clear pathways for students to what matters most in the undergraduate experience.

Academic advising perhaps best illustrates the power of these institutional pathways. Research demonstrates that undergraduates at all different institution types "who reported talking to an academic adviser either 'sometimes' or 'often' had significantly higher persistence rates than those who did not," and gains are greatest for first-generation and low-income students (Klepfer & Hull, 2012, pp. 10–11). For advising relationships to reach full potential, however, students and advisers must do more than efficiently complete the course registration process. Advising conversations should be moments of reflection about a student's goals and challenges, helping the student both to understand and navigate the curriculum and integrate individual college experiences into a coherent vision of the student's future (Drake, Jordan, & Miller, 2013). Marc Lowenstein notes that "an excellent adviser does for students' entire education what the excellent teacher does for a course" by helping them to see the undergraduate experience as more than a collection "of discrete, isolated pieces but instead as a unity, a composition of interrelated parts with multiple connections and relationships" (quoted in Folsom, Yoder, & Joslin, 2015, p. 15).

To fulfill that potential, institutions need to take responsibility for shepherding students along pathways to meaningful relationships. Many institutions boast of having excellent programs, but that is not sufficient for students to have excellent undergraduate experiences. As Chambliss and Takacs (2014) conclude, "What matters ... is who meets whom, and when. Programs succeed only when they bring the right people together. If the right people are involved, a variety of curricula can serve colleges well. If they aren't, no curriculum will work" (p. 157).

Nurture Both Learning and Belonging Through Relationships

The academic dimensions of undergraduate relationships often seem clear and straightforward: A faculty member teaches the student how to do something, such as conduct a literature review, formulate a research question, collect and analyze data, or prepare for a professional presentation. But the psychosocial dimensions of these relationships are equally important to a student's growth and development. Research by Terrell Strayhorn (2012) and others demonstrates that a sense of belonging is vital to student learning and success for a diverse range of undergraduates. Strayhorn defines belonging as "the experience of mattering or feeling cared about, accepted, respected, valued by, and important to the group (e.g., campus community) or others on campus (e.g., faculty, peers)" (p. 3). Belonging is always relational, bridging the gap between the individual and the group. A sense of belonging can be culti-vated in students (and others on campus) through practices including setting clear expectations for success, establishing trust, maintaining strong and regular communication, giv-ing honest feedback (even when difficult), and celebrating milestones and accomplishments (Miller, 2015; Vandermaas-Peeler, 2015).

Experienced advisers and mentors know how to scaffold experiences for students so that they encounter increasing levels of challenge, are encouraged to take greater intellectual risks, and emerge from the process with both higher levels of indepen-dence and a firm sense of being part of an academic community. Effective mentors also know how to foster student-to-student relationships in communities of practice (Lave, 1991) organized around a particular interest or research area, such that more experienced students guide and inspire their more novice peers and in turn contribute to a culture of support and challenge in an academic department, a co-curricular program, or an on-campus job (Newton & Ender, 2010). These grassroots efforts, sometimes with an inspiring adviser or mentor at the epicenter, can connect generations of students and alumni to an intellectually rigorous and supportive community of learners on campus.

For instance, in well-known research on calculus students at Berkeley, mathematician Uri Treisman (1992), looking to understand differences in student performance, compared the study habits of Black calculus students with those of Chinese students. Treisman found that although Black students worked diligently, they studied mostly in isolation. The Chinese students, in contrast, reviewed homework assignments together, checked each other's answers, and discussed problem sets over meals. Seeing this, Treisman offered Black students an intensive workshop environment in addition to the regular class, "emphasizing group learning and a community life focused on a shared interest in mathematics" (p. 368). The results were dramatic, with Black students who studied with peers performing comparably to all of their classmates in calculus. Treisman then developed a widely replicated pedagogy that emphasized to all students "that success in college would require them to work with their peers, to create for themselves a community based on shared intellectual interests and common professional aims" (p. 368). (For a synthesis of more recent research on this type of pedagogy, see Drane, Micari, & Light, 2014.)

The Collegia Program at Seattle University aims for a similar outcome through a very different approach. On many campuses, transfer and returning students report feeling isolated and not fitting in, although many of these nontraditional students bring academic and life experiences to college that would enrich the educational environment for all (Silverman, Aliabadi, & Stiles, 2014). The Collegia Program creates home-like environments for cohorts of transfer, commuter, and returning students. Each

Collegium Community has a convenient and comfortable physical location (including study and casual hangout spaces), a staff of students who welcome and serve as resources to their peers, and a designated student population, such as military veterans or juniors and seniors in the sciences, engineering, and nursing (Seattle University, n.d.).

Both the Collegia Program and Treisman's (1992) findings on the power of study groups beg the question about how much student failure in higher education—across racial and ethnic differences, across socioeconomic differences, across disciplines, and more—can be attributable to student isolation and the lack of peer communities to support learning. What we do know is that relationships matter in part because they help students to learn and to feel that they belong in college.

Encourage Everyone on Campus to Cultivate Relationships

Although most of this chapter has focused on peer-to-peer and student–faculty relationships, other members of a college or university community also have profound roles to play in students' development. Athletics coaches teach valuable lessons about persevering, overcoming adversity, developing a strong work ethic, performing as a team, and pursuing excellence through ongoing practice. Campus work supervisors mentor students in workplace professionalism and teach them valuable lessons through their interactions with the public. Members of the alumni body can serve as mentors on subjects such as transitioning to one's first job and understanding a workplace or internship culture. And, of course, student affairs staff in residence life, orientation programs, the judicial office, and student activities can positively shape students' daily lives as advisers, mentors, and counselors. Every person on a college campus has the potential to be a teacher and mentor, and all should be supported by strong institutional expectations and commitments.

Students often know this already, and at many colleges students can readily identify certain staff members who have influence on the campus culture that far outweighs their institutional roles. At Wofford College in South Carolina, for example, one such person is Rita Rillman. Miss Rita, as everyone calls her, supervises the Acorn Café, a small coffee shop on campus. Through her daily interactions with students, Miss Rita has become an informal counselor to many students. Stories abound about her sage advice and her persistent encouragement. Students routinely introduce their parents to Miss Rita (Kuh, Kinzie, Schuh, Whitt, & Associates, 2010), and someone has even created a Pinterest site where alumni and current students can sing her praises. When Wofford's new president, Nayef H. Samhat, gave his first convocation address in 2013, he mentioned only two Wofford-affiliated people by name, the student government president and Miss Rita (Samhat, 2013). Staff like Miss Rita carry out the institution's mission by supporting and challenging students to be their best and cultivating each student's sense of belonging by communicating that someone notices and cares.

Institutions can systematically develop this kind of ethic of care not only by paying careful attention to human resources but also by developing practices and structures that foster relationships (Blimling & Whitt, 1999). Elon University has a long tradition of College Coffee, a 40-minute time every Tuesday morning when no classes are held so that everyone on campus is available to gather for coffee and conversation. College Coffee provides a pleasant and informal opportunity for students, staff, and faculty to interact. The precise outcomes of this practice are impossible to quantify, but many on campus—and many alumni—cherish the spirit of community and connection that emerges from College Coffee (Johansson & Felten, 2014).

Physical space and architectural design also can be powerful tools to facilitate relationships and belonging. As campus planner Daniel R. Kenney and colleagues write, "If we design our buildings and spaces in certain ways, we can cause certain things—more effective learning, more vibrant community—to happen there" (Kenney, Dumont, & Kenney, 2005, p. 4). Imagine how intimidating it can be for a reticent first-year student to walk down a long corridor of closed doors on the way to a faculty member's office for the first time. Now imagine that same student stepping into an inviting space where faculty and students are talking in pairs and small groups, adjacent to a cluster of faculty members' offices. Welcoming collegiate spaces can encourage conversation and interaction after class, in dining halls, and in the evening. Hampden-Sydney College in Virginia has created casual outdoor gathering spaces near every campus residence. These highly visible spaces are frequent meeting places for faculty, staff, and students making apparent the relationships that often are hidden away in offices and conference rooms on many campuses. Careful design like this can make a world of difference in communicating the value of personal relationships in the collegiate experience.

Celebrate and Reward Relationship Building

Colleges and universities typically give major awards for distinguished teaching and scholarship, but it is less common to recognize excellence in the kinds of activities that most contribute to meaningful relationships. On many campuses, faculty and staff doubt (often for good reason) that institutional pronouncements about the significance of being an effective academic adviser, mentoring undergraduate research, or even having lunch with students will actually count in the promotion, tenure, and annual review processes. By publicly acknowledging and rewarding the importance of professional work that leads to the creation and support of educational relationships on campus, leaders, including deans and chairs, can make important statements about institutional priorities and values.

At many colleges and universities, faculty efforts toward relationship building do not fit neatly into one of the traditional categories of teaching, scholarship, and service. Undergraduate research and academic advising, for instance, might be framed as part of a faculty member's teaching responsibilities, but neither of these activities appears on student evaluations of teaching, which often are the primary (or the only) measure of teaching effectiveness. Even at institutions with more robust approaches to teaching evaluation, faculty typically are rewarded for individual excellence rather than for collaborating with peers and students (Felten & Finley, 2013). The University of Louisville's annual Paul Weber Award for Departmental Excellence in Teaching illustrates how a large research institution can create incentives for meaningful relationships. The $30,000 Weber Award recognizes an academic department or unit on campus that works collegially and collectively on teaching and learning. Both the monetary size and the campus profile of the Weber Award create strong incentives for faculty to collaborate (University of Louisville, 2015).

Recognition and rewards can be meaningful, of course, even when they are not accompanied by large checks. Rollins College in Florida has an online Wall of WOW that allows anyone in the community to acknowledge individual acts of service excellence including those that demonstrate the ethic of care that supports relationships and belonging. A simple web-based form is used to gather nominations, which are forwarded to the person's supervisor and are posted to the wall for all to see. A quick glance at the wall (Rollins College, 2015) conveys the campus norms of service and community. Custodians, librarians, campus security officers, information technology staff, and many others are singled out for specific praise. One nominator, for instance, names several colleagues who were "joyful, hard-working, thoughtful, present, resourceful, [and] caring" during a particularly stressful week on campus (February 26, 2015). Rollins complements these individual WOWs with a Service Excellence Award for departments or teams that effectively enact the college's mission and values; winners of this award each receive a $10 gift card and, more importantly, public acknowledgment at an annual campus ceremony.

One of the most serious impediments to building an institutional culture that is committed to fostering strong relationships is the increasing reliance by many institutions on part-time faculty and staff, especially for instruction in first-year, general education courses in which students are most in need of advising and mentoring and where students are least likely to feel a sense of belonging. At the same time, many financially strapped institutions have aimed to attract and keep students by enhancing campus amenities like dining halls, recreation centers, and sports teams (Strayhorn, 2012). Although these can be effective tools for retaining students and building institutional loyalty, the academic heart of the undergraduate experience requires an investment in a permanent faculty and staff—everyone from full professors to Miss Rita—who are uniquely positioned to mentor and advise students through their educational journeys in college.

Conclusion: Relationships at the Heart of College

In her book *Big Questions, Worthy Dreams*, Sharon Daloz Parks (2011) calls us to think of the purposes of relationship building beyond preparing students for successful careers or graduate study:

> For many reasons, the practice and wisdom of mentoring has been weakened in our society. We compensate for this loss with a professionalism that is too often delivered without the "life-giving, caring field once provided by elders." But this has contributed to fragmentation and loss of transcendent meaning, for which no amount of professional expertise can compensate. Restoring mentoring as a cultural force could significantly revitalize our institutions and provide the intergenerational glue to address some of our deepest and most pervasive concerns. (pp. 13–14)

Higher education could indeed be substantially improved if we paid more attention to the importance and quality of mentoring and relationships in undergraduate education. In his recent study of programs that nurture a sense of purpose and vocation in students, Tim Clydesdale (2015) concludes that essential elements of this work include "intellectual substance" and "sufficient time to foster interpersonal connections" focused on "the most receptive moments in a student's or employee's life course" (pp. 195, 213).

This will not be easy. Many aspects of contemporary American collegiate life work against building a culture that forges strong and positive faculty–student and peer-to-peer relationships. The plagues of sexual violence and binge drinking, for instance, cause great damage to individuals and groups, diminish every dimension of campus life, harm students' academic performance, and make healthy interpersonal relationships difficult to sustain. Other significant barriers include the pressing need for many students to spend considerable time working in order to afford college, a commuter culture where students are not engaged with faculty or each other outside class, and the difficulty some students, like performing arts majors and athletes, have scheduling semester-long high-impact practices into their very demanding schedules.

A strong commitment to nurturing meaningful mentoring and advising will be necessary to counter these powerful forces and to approach Parks's (2011) aspirations for relationships in the academy. Ironically, the surest path toward hard outcomes like retention and graduation rates may well be through the soft skills that cultivate relationships and nurture a sense of belonging for all of our students. Indeed, at a time when the value and cost of undergraduate education are routinely being questioned, colleges and universities must offer more than a promise of increased lifetime earnings. The true value of a college or university education includes the number and quality of deep and lasting relationships that contribute to human transformation and the identification of meaning, purpose, and direction in life.

Questions for Reflection

1. How does your institution create structures, environments, and programs to encourage meaningful relationships? Who do these structures and programs tend to involve, and who typically is not included? What could be done to broaden and expand participation beyond these individuals and groups?

2. Are there systemic organizational barriers on your campus that inhibit an integrated approach to relationship building?

3. Which programs and practices best foster the development of strong relationships between students and faculty on your campus? What programs at other institutions might work on your campus?

4. What are the most important and effective practices your institution uses to encourage healthy interactions between students and their peers?

5. Are meaningful relationships with students integrated in areas across your institution, such as academic affairs, athletics, and student life, or through supervision of student employment?

6. How are positive relationships supported, rewarded, and recognized on your campus?

4

EXPECTATIONS MATTER

The scene is the Atlantic Ocean, 130 nautical miles off the coast of North Carolina. Windy gusts of rain streak across the deck of the *U.S.S. John Stennis*, a huge nuclear-powered aircraft carrier, as the air boss and mini boss coordinate flight operations from the bridge. After an F-14 Tomcat, afterburners glowing, is catapulted into the darkness, 150 men and women leap into action, preparing to receive and launch another aircraft, using only hand signals to coordinate a multitude of challenging tasks under harsh conditions. The average age of the crew on deck matches that of the sailor who is steering the ship—19. Standing in the bridge, Charles Schroeder couldn't help but wonder how many students on his campus would have the confidence, self-discipline, determination, and self-reliance to assume such an awesome responsibility. When Schroeder asked a young Marine guard on the ship about this, he responded, "The Corps transformed me. It taught me values, not just words. Honor, courage, commitment, fidelity, integrity. Not just using them, but practicing them. Out in the civilian world those words don't get mentioned."

Although many of these values and virtues actually do appear in our institutional mission statements, how central are they on our college campuses? Do our graduates learn about them and develop the capacity to live by them? If not, why not? Could we acculturate our students to the ethos of our college or university and achieve the same level of dedication and capacity that Schroeder witnessed that day aboard a ship in the Atlantic?

One essential step toward that aim is to recognize and systematically act upon the power of expectations. The military does just that. From drill instructors to generals, military leaders embrace the belief that human beings are much more capable than they think they are, and the leader's role is to actualize that potential to the fullest. Military personnel also are taught that most human limitations are self-imposed and hence can be overcome by clear, consistent, and high expectations for performance improvement.

Decades of psychological research confirm this—people often become what others expect them to become. In Rosenthal and Jacobson's (1968) classic Pygmalion in the Classroom studies, teachers who believed their students were capable of high achievement behaved in ways that helped produce that achievement. The key lesson from research on expectations (Jussim, 2013) is that performance is determined in part by what one believes about people and by one's ability to motivate them to achieve excellence, whether in the classroom, on the playing field, on a residence hall floor, during an advising session, or in a meeting. Expect more, and you'll get more! Another way of stating this is that if all of us—faculty, staff, administrators, board members, and others—believe our students and colleagues can achieve at high levels, if we have aspirational expectations for ourselves and for them, and if we make extra efforts to help them succeed, we often will see phenomenal results.

Expectations, however, are not simply vague wishes or hopes pronounced by people in positions of authority. Research conducted by scholars including Claude Steele (1997) and Darnell Cole (2008) demonstrates that the way expectations are communicated is crucial in shaping behavior and achieving the desired results. Generic positive bromides (e.g., "Do your best work" or "Think creatively") offer limited direction and can be interpreted as patronizing, particularly by students or staff who feel marginalized in higher education. Articulating high, specific, and, as much as possible, individualized expectations while simultaneously conveying an inclusive message of belonging most effectively supports all in succeeding (Steele, 2010). For instance, telling a first-year class that "past students who worked hard tended to succeed in this class" may have little impact on student behavior; however, the same message framed differently can have many more positive results: "I am going to challenge each of you to work hard and learn a lot all semester long, but I know that all of you will succeed in this course if you complete all of the assignments before class, discuss with your peers and me in class, and ask for help when you have questions or are confused."

Although there is long-standing agreement concerning the important role that expectations play in student and institutional performance (Chickering & Gamson, 1987; Study Group on the Conditions of Excellence in American Higher Education, 1984), why are levels of student learning, time to degree, retention and graduation rates, quality service, and other indicators of effectiveness not consistently where we want them to be? The answer might be in part that colleges tend to take everyone's commitment to set and achieve high expectations for granted; that is, institutional leaders assume that students, faculty, and staff know what's important and have clear pathways for achieving these outcomes. However, expectations cannot be taken for granted and must be made explicit.

Expectations Matter: Action Principles

1. Focus expectations on what matters most to student learning and success.

2. Communicate, and reiterate, high expectations.

3. Set expectations early.

4. Implement policies and practices congruent with espoused expectations.

5. Help individuals and groups develop the capacity to set and meet their own expectations.

Focus Expectations on What Matters Most to Student Learning and Success

Establishing and communicating appropriate expectations start with defining what really matters—what is of central importance in undergraduate education to the institution, academic and student life programs, faculty, academic advisers, residence hall directors, and various service providers and to students, families, and others. Not surprisingly, expectations vary considerably within and between these diverse stakeholders. Disconnects often exist about fundamental expectations such as the purposes of college and the ways students should spend their time (Kuh, Kinzie, Schuh, Whitt, & Associates, 2010).

Some of these differences emerge from the roles and responsibilities of different groups on campus. For example, faculty typically value the many things associated with academic learning, including their disciplines, courses, scholarship, and majors, whereas student affairs professionals often most value the co-curricular programs and campus services that contribute to student development.

Even when agreement exists, the way an institution communicates what matters to prospective students is often contrary to its own expectations. Many college viewbooks and websites, for instance, contain glossy images of state-of-the-art recreation centers, impressive dining halls, spacious housing, and attractive students cheerfully interacting with one another on well-maintained grounds on sunny, fall days. Such materials rarely reference academic rigor or the need to work much harder in college than was necessary in high school (Hartley & Morphew, 2008; Slaughter & Rhoades, 2004). No wonder, then, that many students (particularly traditional undergraduates attending residential institutions) arrive on campus with expectations that are primarily focused on social life; they have yet to learn, let alone be told by the institution, about their need to hit the books or ponder big questions of meaning and purpose (Clydesdale, 2008; Miller, Bender, Schuh, & Associates, 2005).

Contradictory expectations can be confusing, sometimes creating wide chasms that shape and distort campus culture. Arum and Roksa (2014), for instance, report in a multi-institutional study that for many students "the importance of the social thus goes much beyond the party scene; it goes to the core of how students define the college experience, understand their purpose in college, and value different dimensions of their college lives" (p. 26). Helping students understand and appreciate academic expectations, then, is not a simple task to be accomplished with a single speech during orientation. Establishing clear, shared norms will require diverse groups on campus working with common purpose but within their own contexts, whether that is a classroom, a convocation, a student group, or a residence hall. This kind of unity without uniformity is possible only if everyone understands what matters most at the institution yet at the same time has opportunities for different pathways toward that desired outcome.

Expectations are based on purpose, values, and personal beliefs at both the individual and institutional levels. Quite simply, our beliefs give birth to our behavior. For example, decades ago the President of Alverno College in Wisconsin, Sister Joel Read, catalyzed an educational revolution when she persistently asked her faculty two simple questions: "What would students miss if they didn't take your class?" and "What should liberally educated people be able to do with what they know?" (Hakel, 1997, p. 18). These questions cut to the core of the institution's purpose and prompted Alverno's faculty to reconsider the relationship between their work and that larger purpose. In other words, to what ends should students, faculty, staff, and others direct their time and energy?

Unfortunately, research demonstrates that students often do not spend their time and energy on educationally purposeful activities (National Survey of Student Engagement, 2015; Schilling & Schilling, 1999, 2005). For more than a decade, scholars and critics have charged that undergraduate education is experiencing a crisis of low expectations often associated with a weak campus culture where students are asked for little and give little in return (Botstein, 2005; Hersh & Merrow, 2005; Keeling & Hersh, 2012). The data too often bear this out. According to the 2015 National Survey of Student Engagement (NSSE), 62% of participating first-year students report spending 15 or fewer hours per week preparing for class (i.e., studying, reading, writing, doing homework or lab work), and seniors report on average spending just under 15 hours per week on similar work. Since, as Alexander Astin (1993) succinctly noted, students learn what they study, no one should be surprised if many students seem to be academically adrift.

The good news, however, is that "when faculty have high expectations, students learn more" (Arum & Roksa, 2011, p. 93). In fact, as Arum and Roksa demonstrate, students perceive that faculty with high expectations also are more approachable than other faculty. In other words, high expectations do not scare students away; they entice students to engage more deeply. The task for institutions, then, is to establish a shared set of clear, high expectations for students—and for others in the campus community.

Communicate, and Reiterate, High Expectations

Having expectations, of course, is not enough. We need to communicate them clearly and consistently to develop a culture of high and focused standards. Although many campuses attempt to regulate behavior through defining what students should *not* do, highly effective campuses take the opposite approach by creating and communicating expectations that reflect the core virtues and values of their institutions. For example, in 1990, the University of South Carolina developed the Carolinian Creed in response to a wide range of student concerns about conduct revealed in a campus culture audit. The creed captures and articulates the university's standards, expectations, ideals, and aspirations: "As a Carolinian, I ... will practice personal and academic integrity ... will respect the dignity of all persons ... will respect the rights and property of others ...." (University of South Carolina, 2015). By framing the creed as a common set of positive values and actions rather than a list of offenses and violations, the university affirms its shared norms.

Because diverse campus constituents contributed to the drafting of the Carolinian Creed, the document is used to articulate institutional expectations throughout the campus—in classrooms, residence halls, Greek organizations, and faculty meetings. The creed is printed in many university publications, from admissions brochures and applications to exam booklets. Framed prints or plaques appear in many offices. In addition, all students sign the Carolinian Creed as a part of their undergraduate admissions application, and inductions of officers for various student groups include it. Faculty who teach first-year students also underscore its meaning and applicability to their classes. Additionally, each fall a Carolinian Creed Day includes an essay contest about the creed and its impact on the campus and individual community members. In the spring, a Creed and Diversity Week is held and most recently included a CreedX luncheon during which faculty, staff, students, and alumni gave short talks on their personal experience with the creed. For over a quarter century, it has helped to significantly improve peer relationships by explicitly communicating expectations and has positively influenced duties and obligations associated with membership in the University of South Carolina academic community.

Other colleges and universities also have moved to make explicit the values, principles, and ethics that reflect what matters most in their own particular communities. Santa Monica College, the first community college in California to formally adopt an honor code, roots its statement in essential principles: Honesty, integrity, social responsibility, and respect and civility. The code of conduct at Wabash College, a men's college in Indiana, is even more succinct: "A Wabash student is expected to conduct himself, at all times, both on and off campus, as a gentleman and a responsible citizen" (Wabash College, 2015). While such brief statements are not guides to specific action, they are helpful and memorable prompts—and they can be excellent starting points for discussions and reflections about what it means to have integrity and to be a responsible citizen.

Students, of course, are not the only ones who benefit from repeatedly reflecting on an institution's high expectations. Staff at Northwestern Louisiana State University (NSU), for example, created a student-centered philosophy statement that is framed and prominently displayed in every campus office:

1. Because NSU students have a need, we have a job.

2. Because NSU students have a choice, we must be the best option.

3. Because NSU students care, we must be considerate.

4. Because we value NSU students' time, we must be quick.

5. Because NSU students are unique, we must be flexible.

6. Because NSU students have high expectations, we must excel.

7. Because of NSU students, we exist (Schroeder, 2012).

This statement reminds staff and everyone else who sets foot on campus about the university's high expectations for all at NSU.

Set Expectations Early

Students' expectations of college are shaped either serendipitously or more purposefully long before students arrive on our campuses. Students enroll with hopes and expectations that their college will deliver every day on its promise to be a certain kind of institution. The greater the degree of congruence between these initial expectations and their experiences, the more likely students will be not only satisfied but also successful (Braxton, Vesper, & Hossler, 1995; Pike, Hansen, & Childress, 2014). And, of course, the same principle rings true for new faculty and staff.

Appropriate expectations can be communicated well before students matriculate. This begins with the first contact between student prospects and institutions. The messages communicated during college fairs and campus visits, and through mailings and webpages, create expectations and implicit promises about what it is like to attend the institution. Take Gonzaga University, for example: It is a Catholic Jesuit institution in Washington State that, like all Jesuit schools, views "forming students for lives of leadership and service for the common good" as its primary mission (Gonzaga University, 2015). It introduces prospective students to the key components of this mission—faith, service, ethics, justice, and leadership—during a spring event, the Gonzaga Experience Live (GEL). The GEL program includes campus and local Spokane community tours, an overnight stay in a residence hall with a current student, interactive academic classes, and in-depth discussions of what it means to live a moral life within the context of a Jesuit community. These conversations introduce students to the ethos of the institution and its major emphasis on academic and co-curricular programs well in advance of the fall semester. About 70% of participants matriculate, and the GEL program is a major contributor to the institution's 93% first-year retention and 74% four-year graduation rates. Like Gonzaga, the University of Notre Dame in Indiana has a robust framework called The Point of It All to orient incoming and first-year students. This year-round program, which begins online before students arrive on campus and continues through the first year, challenges each student to develop the "habits of heart and mind" necessary to succeed in and beyond college and to find a path through the university "that reflects their unique purposes and passions" (University of Notre Dame, 2015).

More typically, references to expectations for academic rigor and the effort required by students to be successful academically are conspicuously absent from campus acclimation efforts. Noticing this hole in its own socialization process, and admiring the programs at Notre Dame and Gonzaga, Elon University recently developed a summer-long online program for new students titled Are You Ready? Incoming students view videos of students and faculty discussing key academic themes and also connect with peers in a handful of interactive online sessions that address issues of interest to new students while also articulating institutional expectations for success. At the end of this summer program, as students are on the verge of coming to campus, the program's title shifts from a question to a statement: You Are Ready. At the incoming class's first in-person gathering, a formal convocation, the theme again focuses on expectations. As the session comes to a close, Elon's president tells students: "We have a date. We'll meet back here in four years for your graduation." The expectations are high and clear, right from the start.

The positive impact of setting high but appropriate expectations is seen across all institutional types from Gonzaga, Notre Dame, and Elon to the Stella and Charles Guttman Community College. In its short history (see Chapter 1), Guttman has achieved remarkable outcomes: Some 30% of new students graduate in two years, and 49% graduate within three years. For the open admissions sector, these rates are impressive, as Guttman's students complete their academic programs at roughly 2.5 times the national norm (National Center for Education Statistics, 2015). One of the elements of the Guttman approach that may explain this success is the institution's attention to setting high, clear, and achievable expectations early and in depth in a required two-week summer bridge program. This huge investment of time devoted to what could generically be called orientation is unusual among community colleges; in fact, many four-year institutions do not require student participation in orientation. The college also makes expectations explicit by providing defined curricular pathways to each major, by having all new students enroll in an interdisciplinary learning community with their cohort from the summer bridge program, and by articulating institutional student learning outcomes that are assessed through students' individual electronic portfolios. A strong peer-mentoring program reinforces a culture of high expectations and student learning. Faculty and staff, including librarians, work together in instructional teams to develop, implement, and assess the curriculum and co-curriculum. This integrated approach surrounds students with clear and high expectations for success.

Implement Policies and Practices Congruent with Espoused Expectations

Although many institutions articulate expectations during orientation, research suggests that too often students' memories fade over time. And students' own expectations of themselves may slide as well. The Wabash National Study has found that students' academic motivation and engagement actually decline during their first year as incoming expectations recede and on-campus realities set in, leading students to study less in subsequent years than they had expected to and to spend more time on nonacademic pursuits (Arum & Roksa, 2011). Expectations cannot be once-and-done but rather must be sustained and reinforced by institutional policies and practices across campus. As we described in Chapter 1, Astin's (1985) theory of student involvement holds that the college environment is essential in shaping student involvement and engagement—and those behaviors directly influence student outcomes.

At Fayetteville State University (FSU), an HBCU in North Carolina, most students are first generation and financially high-need, and some are not well prepared academically when they arrive on campus. Also, many have connections to the military because the 82nd Airborne Division of the U.S. Army is quartered at nearby Ft. Bragg, which gives FSU a particularly diverse and transient student population. FSU faculty and staff calibrate their expectations to high yet attainable levels, aiming to develop what Stanford psychologist Carol Dweck (2006) calls a "growth mindset" in students. According to Dweck's research, people with a "fixed mindset" assume that qualities like intelligence or talent are established traits that cannot be meaningfully altered: Either you're born with them, or you're not. A growth mindset, on the other hand, considers innate intelligence or talent to be a starting point and emphasizes that abilities can be cultivated through hard work and dedi-cation. Translating Dweck's research into practice, faculty in FSU's first-year writing courses offer students opportunities to submit essays multiple times until they meet the desired performance standard. This not only gives students chances to work toward a high standard, but, equally important, it enhances their intellectual self-confidence by helping them see that growth is possible through persistence and struggle. This practice illustrates a key principle about expectations: Meeting high standards is a source of motivation, accomplishment, and increased confidence (Cole, 2008; Dweck, 2006). But if expectations are too high, students may become frustrated and overwhelmed. Conversely, if expectations are too low, boredom and inactivity may result. FSU bases its educational practices on a fundamental assumption about learning: Students need to be both challenged and supported, with an appropriate degree of balance between the two.

Expectations at FSU extend beyond the traditional classroom. Starting with the first-year seminar, students are required to participate in weekly professional preparation days where they come to class in business attire and deliver brief speeches to classmates. This is reinforced in the career center where students learn not only how to prepare resumes and cover letters but also proper etiquette for dinner meetings and other formal business occasions. For many first-generation college students, such guidance is both practical and aspirational. The message from FSU is explicit: We expect students not only to be academically successful but also to be prepared to interact effectively in the world of work.

Unfortunately, many campuses do not demonstrate this commitment to setting high expectations. At colleges and universities across the country, we have heard faculty and staff respond to evidence that their students lack engagement in important educational experiences and campus services, such as undergraduate research or tutoring, by saying something like, "But those experiences and resources are available to students, and we list them online." Simply detailing opportunities for engagement online does not constitute a meaningful contribution to student learning and success. On the contrary, effective colleges do not leave engagement in powerful educational experiences to chance or solely to student initiative. They provide clear expectations and pathways that prompt and guide meaningful involvement.

For instance, in response to lower-than-desired four-year graduation rates, the University of Houston (UH) created a program called UH in 4 that is designed to provide such pathways. UH in 4 starts with the expectation, appearing across campus on everything from posters to T-shirts, that students will graduate in four years. The program's tagline emphasizes that both individual students and the institution have roles to play: "You're going places; we'll help you get there." UH in 4, however, is more than a slogan. It also guarantees a four-year graduation for a student who takes at least 30 credit hours per year, meets with academic advisers each semester, follows the course sequence in the academic map, monitors degree progress, remains in good academic standing, and notifies the university of course unavailability.

Creating expectations and tools for timely degree completion has been an effective tool for many other institutions as well. For years, Lynchburg College in Virginia and Hendrix College in Arkansas have registered all their students for the full academic year rather than semester by semester. This registration policy communicates, especially to new students, that these institutions expect them to be enrolled all year. Similarly, Tennessee Tech Centers, a group of seven state institutions focused on workforce development, have increased completion rates by redesigning their registration systems so that students now sign up for entire academic programs rather than on a course-by-course basis. Other institutions are developing equally innovative strategies for reducing costs by streamlining the time to a degree. Advisers at San Diego State University explicitly state the expectation that all students will register for full course loads every term. Duke University encourages students to create concrete four-year plans using online tools that prompt them to consider double majors, study abroad, and other opportunities; the system then monitors student progress and future course availability, notifying students when they get off track. Finally, public institutions in Complete College America (CCA), a national nonprofit organization that works with states to significantly increase the number of Americans with college degrees or certificates, are providing guided pathways that determine what courses students should take and when.

Of course, clear expectations and pathways are not always enough to keep students on track. Dropping out even as late as the senior year is surprisingly common, especially in institutions with large enrollments of transfer, nontraditional, and part-time students. Unlike students who tend to drop out in the first two years, most of these seniors are in good academic standing and only a few credits short of degrees. In 1996, to address this phenomenon, the University of New Mexico created the Graduation Project, a program that each summer identifies all the students, including many seniors, who have left the university in the previous year in good academic standing and with at least 98 credits. These students then are offered a simplified reenrollment application, small financial grants, and advocates who can help them address any reenrollment challenges. To date more than 2,500 have returned to the university and completed their undergraduate degrees because of the Graduation Project. Although these students had gotten off track initially, the university persisted in acting on its expectation that students want to graduate and created an effective program to make graduation possible for more of its students (University of New Mexico, 2015).

Help Individuals and Groups Develop the Capacity to Set and Meet Their Own Expectations

Articulating clear expectations and effective pathways not only facilitates time to degree, student satisfaction, and other desired outcomes but also helps undergraduates develop the essential capacity of establishing and monitoring progress toward their own expectations. This capacity, which scholars call metacognition, is a necessary step toward becoming a lifelong learner, a common goal higher education institutions set for students. To develop metacognitive abilities, students need repeated opportunities to practice a series of related steps: Assessing a challenging task; evaluating their own strengths and weaknesses related to that task; planning and taking action; monitoring their progress and adjusting their actions as appropriate; and, finally, replacing on what they learned from tackling this challenge (Ambrose, Bridges, DiPietro, Lovett, & Norman, 2010).

Students develop metacognitively in courses and co-curricular activities, but too often it is haphazard and unguided. In a large study (Bryant, 2014), students across institutional types reported that they did not receive the kinds of timely and ongoing feedback that would most help them learn. Some institutions, for instance, rely on midterm grades both to identify struggling students and to guarantee that students are receiving the guidance they need to succeed in their courses and develop metacognitively. Unfortunately, midterm grades occur too late in the semester for many students, and on many campuses faculty do not take them seriously as an opportunity to support student learning.

The Transparency in Teaching and Learning in Higher Education project based at the University of Nevada at Las Vegas aims to help students develop their own capacities to navigate academic courses by prompting faculty to be explicit about their expectations on assignments. Drawing on research at seven institutions that involved more than 25,000 undergraduates, the Transparency project encourages faculty to answer three questions for students about each of their assignments:

- Task: What exactly are students being asked to do?
- Purpose: Why are they asking students to do this?
- Criteria: How will each student's work be evaluated? (Berrett, 2015)

These three questions are not intended to cause faculty to radically rethink their assignments or their pedagogy, nor do they require expensive technology or elaborate training. However, they have been demonstrated to help students, particularly first-generation undergraduates, to develop what Tara Yasso (2005) refers to as "navigational capital," or the ability to function effectively within academic environments by understanding the implicit rules of the game. Research also indicates that these three transparency questions are particularly powerful because they help faculty state their expectations in ways "that are specific to discipline, class size, level of expertise, and student demographics" (Winkelmes, 2013).

Besides making expectations *of* students clear, institutions also should articulate high and specific expectations of their own performance *to* students. For instance, at Georgia Institute of Technology (Georgia Tech), a service audit revealed considerable variability in the responsiveness and quality of maintenance in the residence halls. This resulted in substantial student dissatisfaction and parental concerns regarding safety and security. To address these challenges, the maintenance department established a set of measurable performance standards and a 24-Hour Response Guarantee and then used campus media, including the student newspaper, to make sure these standards were widely known. Students were assured that within 24 hours of receiving a work order request about a residence hall room, maintenance personnel would visit the student's room to determine the nature of the problem. If minor, a repair would be made at that time. If more time was needed to order a part or bring in a specialist, the maintenance mechanic would leave a hang tag on the door that explained the situation: "I need to order a valve and I will return tomorrow afternoon to install it. Thanks for your patience, Bert." After Bert completed the repair the next day, he would leave another hang tag letting the student know that the job had been completed. Within another 24 hours, a work-study student employee would call the student and say, "I'm calling on behalf of the director of housing; he just wants to make sure that the maintenance repair was done to your satisfaction." This call emphasized more than anything else that this student and his or her satisfaction mattered. This process of defining service excellence in terms of clear performance standards and measuring and providing feedback on those standards transformed the residence hall maintenance system and in the process humanized a part of the student experience.

Service excellence initiatives such as the one at Georgia Tech have many institutional benefits. They establish a clear aim that focuses expectations for efforts on what matters in every transaction—responsive, respectful, and competent service. They demonstrate staff members' commitment to one another and to their stakeholders by providing common ground for teamwork and collective effort. And they provide a platform for continuous improvement based upon clear and measurable service standards developed and embraced by each service unit.

Conclusion

Student success should not be left to chance. It requires an ongoing process of communicating institutional expectations and values and then of aligning those with action through appropriate policies, processes, and high-impact practices—not only for students but also for faculty and staff. By setting high expectations for everyone and also delivering on promises, the full potential of both individuals and institutions is realized.

Every institution needs to have an intentionally crafted common message communicating a set of expectations, values, and practices that entering and continuing students hear clearly and repeatedly from faculty, staff, administrators, and peer leaders. Usually these messages include statements of what we expect students to do and why and the benefits to them for doing so. The message communicates the institution's core values to all constituencies.

We know that when it comes to whether our expectations are realized, we often get what we predict. Unfortunately, some individuals and institutions continue to hold to the implicit assumption that students who struggle are just not college material. However, both higher education research and institutional examples consistently demonstrate that this is simply not the case. When students are challenged with high expectations and then are systematically supported with people, pedagogies, and resources, success is possible. Indeed, we should expect nothing less from all of our students.

Questions for Reflection

1. What are the expectations that your institution explicitly communicates to students, faculty, and staff? What are the implicit expectations the institution communicates? How do the explicit and implicit expectations align?

2. How clear, consistent, coherent, and explicit are expectations for different constituent groups (that is, students, staff, faculty) at your institution? How are those expectations linked to your institution's mission and values and focused on students and learning? Where and how are these communicated?

3. Are expectations for student performance set at appropriately high levels, given students' academic preparation? Are academic challenges for students balanced with appropriate support?

4. How do you and your institution encourage and support individuals and groups in setting and meeting their own expectations?

5. What methods (for example, honor codes, traditions, rituals, formal events, trainings, social media) does your institution use to uphold, reinforce, and celebrate expectations?

6. How do you address gaps between desired institutional expectations and actual performance?

5

ALIGNMENT MATTERS

J ust as the great recession tore into the economy in 2008, the University of South Carolina (USC) began to lay the foundation for an ambitious new initiative: USC Connect. Financial issues derailed many other plans, but this one stayed on track because it complemented ongoing general education revision and strategic planning at the university by aligning undergraduate learning experiences within and beyond the classroom. USC Connect promotes student engagement in both purposeful experiences and guided reflection on the meaning of those experiences. It emphasizes four learning pathways outside the classroom: Community service; global learning (e.g., study abroad); research; and professional and civic engagement, which includes peer leadership and internships. Starting with a first-year seminar, University 101, students are challenged to learn in integrative ways and to use e-portfolios to document the products of and reflections on their learning experiences in and out of class. USC Connect staff, based in the Office of the Provost, collaborate with professionals in student affairs and other offices sponsoring experiences (e.g., study abroad, undergraduate research) to promote systematic student reflection. USC Connect staff also work with faculty to increase opportunities for integrative learning in academic courses and programs.

USC Connect allows students to earn Graduation with Leadership Distinction (GLD) in community service, global learning, research, or professional and civic engagement. The honor is published on both transcripts and diplomas. GLD requirements vary, but each includes significant beyond-the-classroom engagement (e.g., 300 hours of community service), related course work, a public presentation, and an e-portfolio demonstrating learning and reflection across experiences. The GLD pilot of 90 students in the first year quickly grew to a registration of over 900 students by the beginning of the third year. Efforts to promote GLD have led to the addition of reflective components in assignments and increased use of e-portfolios as a vehicle to integrate learning. A universally available senior seminar, University 401, which bookends the first-year seminar, uses e-portfolios as a signature assignment and grew from one section the first year to fourteen sections a year later. Assessment results have prompted new targeted efforts to better support students in making the most challenging connections, such as how to use what they have learned to inform their personal and professional decision making.

USC Connect is an ambitious and comprehensive example of intentional alignment, an often-elusive goal for higher education institutions. Alignment involves matching resources, policies, and practices with the institution's educational purposes and student characteristics through forging educational partnerships within and among traditional organizational boundaries, especially faculty, academic affairs, and student affairs units (Kuh, Kinzie, Schuh, Whitt, & Associates, 2010). It is not a new concept in higher education, and many accrediting bodies expect institutions to show evidence of alignment among their mission, vision, values, strategies, and actions. However, alignment is more common in theory (and in accreditation reports!) than in practice. Actual alignment requires that policies, practices, and processes be integrated in a seamless fashion, melding once distinct parts into a coherent whole.

Although alignment may appear simple, it can be a vexing aspiration for academic cultures (Bergquist & Pawlak, 2007; Kellogg Commission, 2000). Colleges and universities often operate as federations of schools, departments, and programs with distinct loyalties and goals related to their individual missions. That complexity makes alignment all the more important for our students and our institutions.

Alignment Matters: Action Principles

1. Make alignment a shared goal.

2. Align administrative practices and policies.

3. Align academic programs and campus practices.

4. Challenge students to align their learning.

5. Leverage the benefits of alignment.

Make Alignment a Shared Goal

Achieving ambitious strategic goals requires that individuals and groups across the institution act in ways that are aligned with a broad vision. As helpful as inspiring rhetoric and catchy slogans are, alignment succeeds best when people see their own interests as linked to institutional aims.

Groups are far more likely to work together if they share a compelling aim and understand that it can be better accomplished through collaborative alignment across the institution. To arrive at this point, institutional leaders must articulate values and mediate diverging opinions about what matters most. Often this can be done by focusing on higher order goals, such as achieving greater levels of student participation in high-impact practices or challenging students to pursue more fully integrated learning experiences.

Alignment also requires new ways of thinking about leadership. Top down, traditional models often need to give way to integrative thinking and action, cooperation and teamwork, and collaboration and functional integration. Creating alignment through educational partnerships is hard work that necessitates everyone being willing to examine deeply held and often divergent assumptions about what matters in undergraduate education and in organizational responsibilities and status. In a nutshell, alignment requires leaders who are willing to function as designers, collaborators, teachers, and stewards. They have to have a vision for the desired alignment and the managerial and leadership skills to actually make it happen.

Effective alignment can be challenging unless constituent groups embrace a mindset that Senge (1990) describes as systems thinking, the capstone of organizational learning. Systems thinking is an approach that shifts the focus from parts and pieces to systems and wholes. If educators and students are to experience a college or university as a purposeful system, we need to do the hard work of aligning and connecting its disparate units and functions.

Many colleges and universities, for instance, require first-year undergraduates to participate in new student orientation, complete certain general education courses, and live in residence halls. These experiences often are conducted and viewed as distinct activities rather than components of an integrated system intentionally designed to support academic and social engagement though alignment and continuity. Some institutions, however, like Newman University in Kansas, align orientation, a first-year seminar, a general education course, a learning community, and first-year advising in a seamless student experience. At Newman each new undergraduate is assigned an adviser who also teaches one of the two linked general education courses and one of the required first-year seminars. By interacting weekly with students in both the seminar and the general education course, advisers form rich relationships with their advisees. In recent years this model has increased fall-to-fall retention by over 10%. In Newman's case, then, alignment across previously separate structures contributed substantially to both institutional goals, such as retention and relationship building, and to individual student outcomes, including learning and belonging.

Align Administrative Practices and Policies

What matters depends on one's assumptions and beliefs and on one's place within the institution. To be sure, colleges and universities are composed of units with diverse purposes, organizational structures, and missions. Their strengths can also be their weaknesses and limitations. According to Karl

Weick (1983), "Universities are highly differentiated and low on integration, with the basic organizational element (faculty) loosely coupled. The high need for independence and accuracy is basically inconsistent and contradictory with organizational needs of common purpose, common reference, and smooth functioning" (p. 24). In view of these realities, the challenge is finding common ground, perhaps a shared vision of educational quality and student success, not in a monolithic sense but rather as an aspiration that motivates and inspires cross-functional coordination and collaboration. Such an opportunity was voiced by Ernest Pascarella and Patrick Terenzini (1995) when they suggested that

> Organizationally and operationally, we've lost sight of the forest. If undergraduate education is to be enhanced, faculty members, joined by academic and student affairs administrators, must devise ways to deliver undergraduate education that are as comprehensive and integrated as the ways students actually learn. A whole new mindset is needed to capitalize on the inter-relatedness of the in- and out-of-class influences on student learning and the functional interconnectedness of academic and student affairs divisions. (p. 32)

This analysis continues to resonate decades later because of the considerable obstacles that inhibit an institution's ability to align, including the persistent challenges of communicating within and across units. Specialization also has led to increased compartmentalization and fragmentation, often resulting in functional silos or mine shafts—the opposite of what is needed for alignment. These vertical structures, though often effective at promoting interaction and even achievement within units, create obstacles to interaction, coordination, and collaboration among units (Keeling & Hersh, 2012).

Several years ago, on the campus of one of the authors of this book, a series of silos led to a student loan disbursement process that unintentionally failed to meet broader institutional goals despite the fact that each of the individual units followed their own so-called best practices. In this case, countless students complained that it took a minimum of two months before they received their financial aid checks. As a consequence, many students could not register for courses because administrative holds were placed on their accounts. Many were even forced to take out emergency loans.

When these students eventually received their funds and were cleared to register, some classes were no longer available, so many students had to go through the advising process again, creating considerable redundant work on the part of advisers, staff, and students alike. Individuals and offices tried on their own to help students, but the fundamental problem could be resolved only by a cross-functional team working together. When the directors from the various offices co-created a new and aligned process, the typical student wait time on a loan dropped from two months to just 19 days, which reduced the number of emergency loans by 70%, improved the cash flow of the institution, and saved the equivalent of three full-time positions.

This example illustrates the costs of misalignment and the potential of alignment. In this case, well-intended staff were doing their jobs effectively but in isolation; they were unable to see how their actions extended beyond the boundaries of their positions and affected the institution's primary goal of student success. As a result, their efforts produced much more waste (e.g., added costs in times of rework, emergency loans) without value (timely, appropriate, and effective registration). Just as these problems are systemic in nature, their solutions need to be systemic. Or, put another way, an organization is like a relay team: The better the handoffs, the better the results (Seymour, 2002). By shifting our focus from insular functions to cross-unit processes and by cultivating a belief that alignment matters, individuals will begin to use boundary-spanning strategies to identify and resolve misalignments. This will pay particularly high dividends when acting on opportunities for alignment (or examples of misalignment) that touch many students, staff, and faculty.

At DePaul University in Chicago, students have benefited from the alignment of enrollment and administrative services. DePaul Central provides a one-stop location for integrated student services in financial aid, student accounts, and student records and registration. Creating and sustaining DePaul Central requires extensive collaboration among six administrative divisions: Enrollment management and marketing, financial affairs, student affairs, facilities operations, information services, and academic affairs. By spanning these boundaries, DePaul Central staff over the past decade have developed systemic solutions to improve overall processes so that students' enrollment experiences are as smooth, pleasant, and seamless as possible. Using a two-tiered service model, 50 DePaul Central staff members are cross-trained to handle the most common concerns of students, leading to over 90% of inquiries being resolved at the first point of contact. That is significant to both students and the institution because, in a recent two-year period, DePaul Central staff had more than 200,000 interactions with students, including some 80,000 that were face to face and more than 120,000 on the phone or online. The efficiency and effectiveness achieved by DePaul Central's alignment makes it the go-to place for students seeking help with administrative questions, and guarantees that those students will receive quick and accurate answers.

Align Academic Programs and Campus Practices

In *The End of College*, Kevin Carey (2015) harshly critiques the hybrid university, an incoherent jumble of competing factions that focuses little attention on undergraduates or teaching. The negative results for students, Carey concludes, are predictable. And the results for colleges and universities will soon be coming home to roost.

Taking a different lens to the same problems, Randy Bass (2012) suggests that undergraduate education in the United States has entered the "post-course era" (p. 24). According to Bass, this disruption has come, somewhat ironically, from within our own institutions. Much of the growth in experiential learning on campuses has developed on the margins of the formal curriculum, creating an unstable situation where a significant amount of learning has little to do with course credits, seat-time, and other traditional measures in higher education: "As a result, at colleges and universities we are running headlong into our own structures, into the way we do business" (p. 24). The problem, Bass concludes, is not that courses and curriculum are fundamentally flawed but rather that institutions and faculty have not done enough to make them the high-impact learning experiences they could and must be.

Aligning academic programs and resources with student learning requires approaching the curriculum, individual classes, and the myriad of other learning structures (from writing centers and tutoring services to academic advising and residence hall programming) as a coherent whole.

One example of comprehensive academic alignment is the first- and second-year program at Christopher Newport University (CNU) in Virginia. CNU's initiative involves several interconnected efforts (Christopher Newport University, 2015):

Calibrating course schedules

Through collaboration among the registrar, director of the Academic Success Center, university fellows, and Core Advisors, entering students receive individualized course schedules to increase the likelihood of their first-term academic success. Two university fellows, recent graduates who serve as full-time engagement advisers, contact all new students at least three times prior to the opening of school to review, update, and in some cases change their schedules to insure an optimal fit with students' background characteristics and educational goals.

Enhancing academic advising

Beginning in the first year, a student works with a faculty core advisor (FCA) who will remain the student's adviser for the first two years (while the student pursues the university core requirements and major prerequisites) even if the student changes his or her area of academic interest. FCAs assist students in their transitions from high school to college, facilitate and encourage students' intellectual explorations and curricular decisions, and challenge students to become active members of the university community. FCAs are required to meet with their advisees five times from summer through the fall term, but only two of the five sessions can focus on course selection and registration. The others emphasize building relationships, successful transitions, engagement in academic support and educational planning, and co-curricular involvement.

Providing early and frequent feedback on student performance

CNU aligns student performance with faculty expectations in first term courses by requiring that students receive in each class a "substantive grade" in the first four weeks of the term. This policy ensures that first-year students have meaningful feedback early enough that they can make changes in their study habits, as appropriate. Since every FCA knows that this feedback is happening, they also prompt students to reflect on and adjust their performance to meet the requirements of their courses.

Supporting a comprehensive early-alert system
This program proactively intervenes with students
needing academic or social support. During summer
preregistration, all students complete the College
Student Inventory, and those identified as at risk
are assigned to staff in the Academic Success Center
(ASC). Any first-year student (at risk or not) who
makes a C– or below in any class at midterm must
meet with staff in the ASC. Faculty teaching first-year
students include a common statement in their syllabi
that stresses the importance of the referral process
to ASC to improve performance in their classes. In
addition, faculty select tutors to work with students in
their classes, creating seamless connections between
faculty and academic support units.

Communicating about resources and strategies
The ASC coordinates frequent communication with
students about both programs and approaches to
support their learning and success. These messages
emphasize the centrality of tutoring, study groups,
and similar activities for students. In addition, staff
created an online program— CLASSified (akin to
CraigsList)—where students can post their academic
needs and connect with peers looking to study together
(e.g., "I am looking for a study group for Chem 123").

**Connecting every student with a residential learning
community**
All first-year students participate in residential learning communities that include enrollment in common

general education courses and assignment to the same residence hall.

The effectiveness of these initiatives comes not from the heroic efforts of isolated individuals but rather from a purposeful and campus-wide commitment at CNU to the educational needs of students. This systematic approach has resulted in a 10% increase in retention and a 20% gain in 6-year graduation rates, and also more student engagement across campus and enhanced academic quality of entering students.

A much larger institution, the University of Texas at Austin, has likewise created an innovative performance improvement program—the Texas Interdisciplinary Plan (TIP)—to bridge the gap between the four-year graduation rates of first-generation students (39%) and students whose parents both graduated from college (60%). This initiative originally began in Chemistry 301, one of the "killer courses" taken by many new students. High-risk students were enrolled in a separate smaller section of Chem 301 that had the same course content, lectures, and tests as the original larger course but also provided a portfolio of aligned student success programs: Peer mentoring, extra tutoring help, engaged faculty advisers, and community-building programs. Through this program, the high-risk first-year students made the same grades and learned as much chemistry as those in other sections of Chem 301 even though there was on average a 200-point difference in their SAT scores! The program model has since been expanded and tailored to different colleges throughout the university (Tough, 2014).

Other institutions like West Virginia Wesleyan College systematically identify high-risk courses that are often prerequisite or gateway courses for particular preprofessional programs such as nursing, allied health, and engineering. The courses are classified as high risk because 30% or more of the grades given are Ds, Fs, or withdrawals (Ws). At West Virginia Wesleyan, the most challenging required course for first-year students is anatomy and physiology, where 50% of students traditionally earned Ds and Fs. Although instructors encouraged students to seek tutoring, the ones most in need rarely did. To remedy this problem, faculty created an Anatomy Boot Camp, which is open five nights a week in the biology department. Faculty teamed with their tutors to provide instruction and encouragement for these struggling students. As a result the number of Fs and Ds dropped from 50% to 29% the first term.

Interdisciplinary team teaching also provides a great opportunity to make direct connections between disciplines by aligning key elements with an overarching goal. One innovative example of such teaching is Southern Utah University's (SUU) The Complete Package, a 34-credit interdisciplinary, general education "mega course" co-taught by eight senior faculty who integrate required classes into one stimulating whole. Courses are taught in blocks that end by noon each day, providing substantial time for students to spend in one or more of SUU's five engagement centers doing academic or co-curricular work linked to course goals. In addition, students participate in off-campus study tours to destinations such as Boston, New York, and Washington, D.C., so they can connect in-class concepts with experiential opportunities outside class. Due to the unique structure of the program, students can complete their entire general education requirements by the end of the first year.

A final example of academic alignment spans even further than an individual department or college. In recent years, many institutions have begun to pay increased attention to the experience of students who transfer from one institution to another, which, in many cases, is far from seamless. That's not the case, however, at the University of Central Florida (UCF), the second-largest university in the nation. UCF's Direct Connect program guarantees entrance and accelerated admission to the university for all students who complete associate's degrees from nearby Brevard, Valencia, Lake Sumter, or Seminole State colleges. High school students enrolling in these colleges can express interest in Direct Connect on their applications and, upon completing their two-year degrees, are automatically admitted to UCF. These students also are encouraged to make four-year academic plans and meet with UCF advisers even when they are enrolled at these regional community colleges. Currently more than 35,000 students are in the Direct Connect pipeline for eventual transfer to UCF, and Direct Connect students graduate at a slightly higher rate than students who start their undergraduate studies at UCF.

Challenge Students to Align Their Learning

We have seen how integrated processes and systems on campuses are important, but alignment is also key for student learning. Institutions should challenge and support all students to synthesize and reflect on their undergraduate experiences to bring them into alignment. This is most likely to happen on campuses that offer programs that encourage integration and meaning making on the individual student level.

A good example of aligning and integrating curricular requirements is the Odyssey program at Hendrix College in Arkansas. Odyssey prompts students to connect what they learn in the classroom with the experience they gain through hands-on learning activities, such as internships, international study, research, and service. Implemented in 2005, Odyssey requires all students to align co-curricular experiences with three approved activities from the following six categories: Artistic creativity, global awareness, professional and leadership development, service to the world, undergraduate research, and special projects. The institution provides grants so that all students can undertake the required projects in these areas. Assessment results demonstrate that Odyssey contributes to four important outcomes for Hendrix students: Learning, professional development, lifelong learning, and civic responsibility (Barth & Gess, 2015).

Of course, the encouragement of reflection, synthesis, and integration of experiences can occur powerfully at the program level as well. Georgetown University has aligned numerous general education courses with co-curricular experiences in the local Washington, D.C. community. Through partnerships with faculty and various external, community-based organizations, the 4th Credit Option for Social Action Program is a Center for Social Justice initiative that provides undergraduate students with additional credits for integrating their academic studies with community engagement experiences. The program is a substantial commitment that requires a student to complete 40 hours of community work over the semester, to write three reflection papers, and to participate in peer dialogue sessions, all in addition to completing the requirements of the classroom instructor. Through the 4th Credit program, students discover how knowledge and action can support and advance one another in the promotion of civic engagement and social justice. The Center then provides multiple opportunities, from informal conversations to annual events, that encourage students to articulate and share what they have learned about themselves, their communities, and social justice.

The power of making alignment explicit and meaningful to students also can be seen in the stories of individual graduates. At her first Elon University Board of Trustees retreat, Aisha Mitchell, one of two holders of young alumni positions on the board, told her fellow trustees about her most transformational experience as a student: Writing a personal statement explaining her educational journey to compete for a highly competitive international fellowship. Through this difficult exercise, Mitchell focused on making meaning of her undergraduate years, integrating her studies in her major and minors, her service, her internships, and her study abroad experiences in China and India. By thinking carefully about how these diverse activities aligned with her own sense of purpose, Mitchell was able to construct a compelling narrative of her undergraduate years and to use this to guide her choices after graduation. Even though she did not receive the fellowship that prompted her reflection, Mitchell found great value in the process of critically reflecting on the connections among and the meaning of her studies and other experiences as an undergraduate.

Leverage the Benefits of Alignment

Effective institutions realize the full educational potential of existing initiatives when they are linked, aligned, and integrated in creative ways. Rather than launching entirely new programs to meet each emerging or lingering need, colleges and universities first should consider whether better alignment of existing resources and efforts could achieve the desired ends.

For instance, although academic advising is a common practice in almost all institutions, Richard Light (2001) contends that "good advising may be the single most underestimated characteristic of a successful college experience" (p. 81). Unfortunately, on many campuses the quality and consistency of the advising varies widely. The roots of this problem are complex but often are linked to limited rewards, absence of a clear aim and purpose, inequitable or unrealistic advising loads, overemphasis on advising as a course selection and registration event rather than an educational planning process, and, perhaps most importantly, lack of alignment with complementary, co-curricular experiences (e.g., internships and academic clubs) designed to promote learning and success. This neglect of quality advising certainly affects, at least to some degree, student engagement, learning, and success. For example, according to the 2014 National Survey of Student Engagement, although first-year students who met regularly with academic advisers reported multiple positive outcomes, about one in three first-years met an adviser only once or not at all during the academic year. And even those who did meet with advisers indicated that they provided little or no information regarding the importance of high-impact practices such as first-year seminars, learning communities, study abroad, and undergraduate research.

To address these kinds of issues, Florida International University (FIU) recently implemented a comprehensive advising program dubbed the Graduation Success Initiative (GSI). The program is new, but the resources and practices involved largely existed on campus already, just not aligned with each other. The program engages students with advisers in a systematic, aligned process that incorporates an initial exploration of majors, an occupational interest inventory that links the students' passions and goals to FIU majors, an automated tracking tool called My eAdvisor that provides students and advisers feedback regarding progression on the Majors Map, and a Panther Degree Audit, which ensures that various steps in the graduation pathway are being met in a timely, appropriate fashion. The GSI not only assures that students will take the right courses in the correct sequence but also exposes students to learning and engagement opportunities on and off campus.

Miami University in Ohio also aligned existing resources to reach a significant goal by linking academic advising with residential life for first-year students. Live-in advisers serve as directors in residence halls that range in size from fewer than 100 to 350 students. Because of the frequent, natural interaction in the dorm, these academic advisers get to know their students on a personal basis and, as a result, engage students in a range of issues that go beyond the traditional emphasis of advising on course selection and registration.

West Virginia University's Adventure West Virginia (AWV) program has had particularly impressive outcomes from aligning existing resources. AVW for years has offered new students four general orientation opportunities (Explore, Wilderness, Habitat, and Odyssey). Through partnerships with faculty and administrators, special AWV programs have been tailored to the distinct goals and needs of academic programs in colleges such as engineering, journalism, and agriculture.

Even though the program began as an adventure orientation program, by aligning with the academic mission of schools and the university, it has become much more. Students who participated in AWV programs between 2004 and 2012, for instance, had significantly higher retention and graduation rates than their non-AWV peers; for students who entered the university classified as at risk, the six-year graduation rate was 26% higher than the general student population. Besides the positive outcomes for individual students, the financial impact of increased retention from AWV participation has been substantial, amounting to nearly $4,000,000 over nine years (Michael & Dueer, 2014).

Conclusion

Intentionally aligning and integrating student and organizational learning is essential for colleges and universities to create meaningful and relevant educational experiences. Thriving institutions do not leave alignment and integration to chance, hoping units and people across campus will coordinate on their own. Nor do they trust that a few key people or boutique programs can foster campus-wide integration. Instead, they seek ways to transform themselves from silos into systems by supporting cross-institution connection and cooperation. Sometimes this requires new or repurposed central integration units such as USC Connect and DePaul Central to do the hard, logistical work of connection and alignment for students, faculty, and staff.

Collaboration is a central element in alignment and the key to making traditional, rigid barriers between our organizational structures more permeable and seamless. By facilitating cross-functional collaboration to forge educational partnerships, especially between academic and student affairs, we can ensure that both student learning and the overall undergraduate experience are not only effective but also, like the experience of the young Marine on the aircraft carrier, transformational.

Alignment begins with our own willingness to leave the comfort of organizational boundaries and familiar practices and to take reasonable risks to champion improved performance—not only for our students but also for our institutions. The challenge thus is not about connecting the fragmented pieces of the student experience; the real challenge is about connecting us.

Questions for Reflection

1. To what extent are curriculum, policies, structures, and resources aligned with your institution's aspirations for undergraduate education? To what extent are your own work and values aligned with your institution's aspirations?

2. Which leaders at your institution are asking hard questions about alignment? Who else could and should be working toward alignment?

3. Do you engage in environmental assessments to identify dysfunctional and misaligned processes? If so, when and how does this work best? If not, how might you begin?

4. How often does your institution challenge prevailing assumptions and take reasonable risks to improve cross-functional processes and programs? How can systems thinking enable your institution to connect the parts to create a better, more holistic experience for students?

5. Are your major institutional processes, such as enrollment and advising, relatively smooth and seamless, or are they misaligned? How effective are the handoffs between key stakeholders in critical process areas?

6. How can you enhance the design and implementation of policies and practices so that they are seamless and agile not only for students but also for staff, faculty, and other key stakeholders?

7. What are the barriers to better alignment on your campus? How can you cultivate perspectives and relationships that will make alignment more possible in the future?

6

IMPROVEMENT MATTERS

I n 2007, with the support of Mayor Michael Bloomberg, City University of New York (CUNY) Chancellor Matthew Goldstein launched a major initiative to address a pervasive problem—consistently low graduation rates among students in the system's community colleges. Backed by major funding from the New York City Center for Economic Opportunity, CUNY invested $19.5 million to create ASAP, Accelerated Study in Associate Programs.

Like many ambitious efforts focused on large-scale improvements, the program's architects started by asking some basic questions: What barriers are preventing students' persistence and how can we remove them? What support do community college students need most to succeed? What is working well that we can build on? Guided by questions like these, ASAP has always had a clear focus; in the words of Donna Linderman, university dean for student success and ASAP executive director, "It all begins and ends with the student" (Linderman, 2016).

Just nine months after Goldstein and Bloomberg announced the program, ASAP launched with a cohort of 1,132 students at six community colleges, providing a set of core program elements: Full-time enrollment, block-scheduled first-year classes, course-taking within cohort groups, increased financial aid, "intrusive and mandatory" advisement, a student-success seminar, career services, and tutoring services. ASAP's leaders emphasized systemic alignment of resources and services. Every detail mattered; because most students were very low income and struggled with the full cost of attending college, ASAP provided critical financial resources to remove barriers to full-time attendance, including free unlimited Metrocards, textbooks, and tuition waivers to cover any gap between financial aid and tuition and fees (Linderman, 2016).

From the outset, ASAP staff committed to being data driven and results oriented and to refine the program model year by year. The results have been impressive for the more than 12,000 ASAP students to date, justifying the plans to scale to 25,000 students by 2018/19 with support from the City of New York:

- ASAP students graduate at more than double the rate of non-ASAP students enrolled at CUNY community colleges (53% vs. 23%);
- That higher graduate rate reflects both ASAP students with developmental needs and those who enter the program fully skills proficient;
- Students from underrepresented groups appear to derive the most benefit from the program;
- After seven years of operation, 64% of ASAP students had earned either associate or baccalaureate degrees as compared to 42% of comparison-group students (ASAP, 2015).

The research firm MDRC recently conducted a five-year random assignment study of ASAP with 900 students from three community colleges who entered with developmental education needs. MDRC found that the three-year graduation rate for ASAP students was nearly double the graduation rate of control group students. MDRC stated that "ASAP's effects are the largest MDRC has found in any of its evaluations of community college reforms" (Scrivener, Weiss, Ratledge, Rudd, Sommo, & Fresques, 2015).

Henry Levin of Teachers College of Columbia University conducted a comprehensive cost-benefit study of the program and found that the cost per graduate for ASAP was lower than for a comparison group (Levin and Garcia, 2012). A cost benefit analysis found that "for every dollar invested in ASAP by the taxpayer, $3.50 is returned per associate degree conferred in the form of increased tax revenues and social services savings, and for each dollar invested by the ASAP student, $12.20 is returned through increased earnings" (Levin and Garcia, 2013).

Programs like ASAP change the life trajectories not only of individual students but also of entire families and communities. One recent ASAP graduate worked as a car service dispatcher before completing his GED and then enrolling in community college to demonstrate the value of an education to his own children. After completing his associate degree through ASAP (while his daughter also was enrolled as an ASAP student), he received a scholarship to earn a four-year degree and now works full time in the Fatherhood Academy at CUNY's LaGuardia Community College (Linderman, 2016).

ASAP is an important example of what can happen when institutions have strong commitments both to improving quantitative institutional outcomes and to improving the individual lives of students and their families through tailored, consistent, student-centered support. ASAP's success illustrates the dynamic relationship between individual and institutional improvement. Students attend CUNY to improve their lives in meaningful ways—their professional prospects, their economic situations, their understandings of the world, their capacities to lead. Although those goals motivate student effort, institutions cannot rely on students alone to carry the burden. Systematic work to improve institutional performance creates environments where students are able to learn and grow. Indeed, a large study of student success in college found that effective institutions are characterized by "positive restlessness," which is "an acculturated wariness that what and how we are doing now can well be improved" (Kuh, Kinzie, Schuh, Whitt, & Associates, 2010, p. 146). This "we can do better" ethos not only works dynamically to improve the institution but also models for students the processes of growth and change.

Improvement Matters: Action Principles

1. Recognize that assessment is fundamental to improvement.

2. Focus assessment on improving what matters most.

3. Commit to using evidence to inform changes.

4. Involve everyone in the process of making change.

5. Adapt best practices from elsewhere.

6. Cultivate an ethos of positive restlessness.

7. Model the process of improvement for students and the institution.

Recognize That Assessment Is Fundamental to Improvement

Understanding is the first step toward improvement. Until you understand what is, you cannot identify a reasonable path toward what could be.

Unfortunately, assessment in higher education too often operates in a culture of compliance. Within this framework, the primary purpose of assessment is to produce results to satisfy external bodies; "instead of faculty members and institutional leaders declaring that improvement of student success and institutional performance was the guiding purpose for documenting student performance—and being encouraged and rewarded for doing so—the interests of others outside the institution" shape what data is gathered and how it is evaluated (Ikenberry & Kuh, 2015, p. 5). Indeed, at some institutions the assessment director is like a modern-day Paul Revere, riding through campus to raise the alarm, "The accreditors are coming! The accreditors are coming!" After marshaling the troops for a formal review, the outsiders retreat and life on the campus green returns to normal. This assessment-for-others orientation has created a chasm between routine assessment practices at many institutions and the people on campus who are most able to act on the results of those assessments to improve student learning—the faculty, staff, and students. Peter Ewell (2009) aptly describes this as the difference between assessment for proving and assessment for improving.

With improvement as the goal, assessment practices can take a wide variety of approaches. Thirty years ago, Richard Light began the Harvard Assessment Seminars as a monthly dinner conversation among colleagues, including faculty and staff from neighboring institutions, along with a sprinkling of Harvard undergraduate and graduate students. Over dinner this group would identify a question about students' collegiate experiences and then create a plan to gather and analyze relevant evidence, often combining institutional data with student interviews or focus groups. At a subsequent dinner, the group discussed the assessment process and results, brainstorming ways to act on what they had found. Over time, this evolving group not only developed more sophisticated understandings of their students and their campuses but also created a number of powerful interventions to improve learning (Light, 2001). Though many assessment initiatives do not occur over dinners with colleagues, all institutions can figure out creative ways to use assessment processes for a larger purpose.

Accreditation is sometimes blamed for the pervasive culture of compliance, but a host of institutions have effectively used accrediting requirements as a lever for improvement (Ewell & Jankowski, 2015). North Carolina A&T State University, for instance, cultivated a culture of inquiry linked to its Southern Association of Colleges and Schools (SACS) reaffirmation processes. The institution's teaching center and its innovative Wabash-Provost Scholars Program brought together faculty and students to examine assessment data, always asking faculty and students, "What do you make of this?" These conversations sparked further research, some of it conducted by trained students, and multiple initiatives aimed at evidence-based improvements in the student experience (Baker, 2012).

By focusing on improving, assessment becomes "problem-specific and user-centered" (Bryk, Gomez, Grunow, & LeMahieu, 2015, p. 12). Those characteristics make it possible for academics to do what they do best, applying their critical capacities to understand and systematically act on complex issues related to both student learning and institutional performance. In other words, assessment as improvement is a key to student and institutional effectiveness.

Focus Assessment on Improving What Matters Most

Assessment can be a powerful lens for improvement, but only when it is focused on what matters most. Effective assessments require clearly articulated goals that are linked to the institution's mission and priorities. Doing this, however, can be difficult. Many institutions have developed complicated systems for collecting and collating data that have little value to the institution. Many residential campuses, for instance, track the number of programs offered by resident assistants without having any evidence that these programs have meaningful outcomes, let alone are attended by many students. As the sociologist William Cameron (1963) noted more than half a century ago, "Not everything that can be counted counts, and not everything that counts can be counted" (p. 13).

With central goals as the focal point, effective assessment collects and analyzes evidence that reflects authentic performance, not isolated data points. St. Olaf College in

Minnesota threads this needle by supporting department-level assessment. When the department of religion sought to assess its students' performance on a core disciplinary and liberal arts goal, the capacity to "form, evaluate, and communicate critical and normative interpretations of religious life and thought," the faculty worked together to evaluate senior essays. When the management studies concentration weighed the merits of team-based pedagogies, which gave students practice with challenging group work but also consumed considerable class time, the faculty compared student performance on individual and group quizzes. In both cases, assessment led to significant improvements, including new writing assignments in religion courses and expanded use of team-based learning in management (Beld, 2010).

While classroom learning is fundamental, in some segments of the campus, such as food service, customer service is a central priority. To improve in this area, targeted assessment is essential. For instance, Campus Dining at the University of Missouri-Columbia uses a mystery shopper program to gather immediate feedback on the quality of daily encounters students have with staff in multiple dining units across campus. Each semester, more than a dozen students are hired and trained to conduct focused, weekly shops and then to provide feedback on the degree to which measurable performance standards are being met from a customer point of view. The standards clearly reflect the department's mission, targeted service objectives, and quantifiable standards that staff helped to create. Feedback from the mystery shoppers is promptly shared with the involved staff, and common themes (both positive and negative) are highlighted in unit-wide communications and trainings. Exemplary stories are shared on the department's Facebook page and through Twitter, reinforcing to staff and students alike that Campus Dining has and meets high standards. This process of systematically gathering and using timely feedback bolsters staff pride and supports a culture of improvement among the staff of Campus Dining—and also models an improvement ethos to students and colleagues across the university (Kiehn, 2015; Schroeder, 2001).

Commit to Using Evidence to Inform Changes

Although institutions have invested vast sums and great hopes in the power of data to serve as a catalyst for change, research demonstrates that evidence alone is rarely sufficient to spark meaningful reform (Banta & Blaich, 2011). Nobel Prize–winning physicist Carl Weiman and his colleagues, for example, conclude that research results seldom are "compelling enough by themselves to change faculty members' pedagogy" in science, technology, engineering, and mathematics (STEM) disciplines (Wieman, Perkins, & Gilbert, 2010, p. 13). Indeed, the authors of a recent meta-analysis found strong evidence that reinforced previous research that students learn more in STEM courses characterized by active learning pedagogies rather than lectures. These authors seemed exasperated when they concluded, "If the experiments analyzed here had been conducted as randomized controlled trials of medical interventions, they may have been stopped for benefit—meaning that enrolling patients in the control condition might be discontinued because the treatment being tested was clearly more beneficial" (Freeman et al., 2014, p. 8413). This problem of individuals and institutions *not* applying what is learned from research is so pervasive in higher education, extending far beyond STEM classrooms, that one of the primary findings from the 49-institution Wabash National Study is that "it is incredibly difficult to translate assessment evidence into improvements in student learning" (Blaich & Wise, 2011, p. 11).

Change is hard, of course, but the human and organizational tendency to remain static may not be sufficient to explain why so little is done with so much evidence in higher education. Charles Blaich and Kathy Wise (2015), building on the work of philosopher Gilbert Ryle, suggest one persuasive explanation. Put simply, they argue that a significant gap exists between "knowing that" and "knowing how." Applying this to the research on STEM teaching, many faculty know that well-executed active learning pedagogies will help their students learn more, but these faculty may not know how to teach in these different ways. Although faculty development programs can change that, STEM faculty at some institutions also might know that teaching innovations are not necessarily a priority in the institutional reward structure, and even at a teaching-focused institution, they may not know how to document their pedagogical innovations for promotion and tenure review. The space between knowledge and execution, in other words, can be a significant barrier to innovation.

Kuh and Hutchings (2015) diagnose another potential cause for the lack of action on assessment data—initiative fatigue. Some campuses and some groups hold tightly to the way they've always done things. However, a larger problem may be that already busy and overstretched colleagues often do not see the value of a new initiative, so they do not know why they should commit to change. Sometimes this is a communications problem, but in large and complex organizations, it often results from hosting multiple programs with competing purposes. Public institutions in Oregon, for instance, recently participated in the Western Interstate Collegiate Commission for Higher Education (WICHE) Passport Project to improve student transfer experiences while simultaneously working to apply the Liberal Education and America's Promise (LEAP) Essential Learning Outcomes (ELOs) and the Valid Assessment of Learning in Undergraduate Education (VALUE) rubrics to high-impact practices. These same universities also joined the Multistate Collaborative Assessment Initiative (MCAI) and received a Lumina Foundation grant to adapt the Degree Qualifications Profile (DQP). Each of these initiatives has the potential to contribute to lasting positive change, but many faculty and staff (or readers of this paragraph!) might reasonably wonder whether and how to engage with this complicated set of overlapping projects (Kuh & Hutchings, 2015, p. 189).

To counter initiative fatigue and to enhance the chances of evidence-based action, institutions and individuals should commit to these five practices (Blaich & Wise, 2011; Kuh & Hutchings, 2015; Walvoord, 2010):

1. Establish clear improvement priorities for sustained focus.

2. Communicate about the educational value and anticipated outcomes of each initiative.

3. Gather enough data to have a reasonable basis for action.

4. Foster conversations about and engagement with that data so that those in positions to act have the opportunity to understand the evidence and shape the actions.

5. Identify and celebrate successes along the way.

Hope College in Michigan used an evidence-based process like this to address National Survey of Student Engagement (NSSE) results that indicated their students did less homework per week than peers at similar institutions. Hope's assessment director presented this data along with other evidence about students' academic efforts, including narrative results from student focus groups, to the full faculty at a dinner meeting. After discussing the meaning of this assessment evidence, faculty decided to have each department develop two specific strategies meant to enhance academic challenge in its courses. Departments reported on their strategies at a campus-wide event, and many faculty changed their teaching to prompt greater student effort. NSSE results from subsequent years demonstrated the effect of this collective effort. Hope students reported significantly more academic effort than on the prior administration of NSSE, and Hope students now compared favorably (in the faculty's eyes) to students at peer institutions in the amount of time they spent doing homework per week (Banta & Blaich, 2011).

Involve Everyone in the Process of Making Change

The University of Maryland–Baltimore County has long used evidence to systematically improve student performance, particularly in the STEM fields. A core strategy has been "the insistence that all groups on campus take ownership of the challenge involving student performance and persistence" (Hrabowski, Suess, & Fritz, 2011, p. 26).

Developing this kind of ownership requires giving a range of groups a voice in shaping both the process and goals of improvement initiatives. Too often, assessment is done to or for people rather than with them. Students, for instance, complete surveys like NSSE or develop portfolios of their best work yet may not know what happens with or as a result of these efforts. Trustees often review assessment reports that provide a lot of information but offer little nuanced or benchmarked evidence to support program oversight or appropriate board action (Sullivan, 2015). To counter this, improvement initiatives should be designed from the start as partnerships among all of the relevant parties.

Effective partnerships draw on the distinct expertise and perspectives of different participants (Cook-Sather et al., 2014). The diversity of the group is an asset, bringing new lenses to see the common work. The Students Assessing Teaching and Learning (SATAL) program at the University of California–Merced illustrates the possibilities of this kind of partnership. SATAL trains and supports a cohort of a dozen or so undergraduates who act as formative assessment consultants to faculty and programs. For instance, SATAL-conducted focus groups with students helped faculty in the applied mathematics program better understand the student experience in their senior capstone, leading to significant improvements in both that course and the curriculum. In another case, SATAL's interviews about student experiences in first-year courses complemented institutional data to support changes in teaching practices across the first year. In these ways, SATAL students not only gather assessment data but also help faculty and programs make sense of that evidence, bringing powerful and informed student voices into important conversations about teaching and learning on campus (Cain & Hutchings, 2015).

The University of Exeter in the United Kingdom has taken this partnership model to a different level with the Students as Change Agents program (Dunne & Zandstra, 2011). This program evolved out of an initiative like SATAL as participants realized the potential of students not simply participating in assessment and improvement activities but also initiating and co-leading such work. Through a number of Staff/Student Liaison Committees (SSLC), Exeter students propose possible projects to improve some aspect of the university. The SSLCs select ideas to pursue and then gather relevant information from diverse perspectives in order to make recommendations for change. Because the SSLCs are supported by institutional resources and embedded within governance structures at the university, significant improvements often emerge, including shifts in pedagogy, curricula, staffing, and student support services.

Adapt Best Practices from Elsewhere

Assessment often focuses internally. That is essential, but institutions also should look externally to identify effective practices at other institutions and within the scholarly literature that could be adapted to meet local goals and needs.

Many students and institutions, for example, struggle with developmental math and statistics. While the particulars vary by campus, common challenges exist including student habits and beliefs that make success unlikely. Drawing on research and a multi-institutional network of faculty, the Carnegie Foundation for the Advancement of Teaching sponsored the creation of a set of strategies to support students in cultivating productive persistence. Both scholarly studies and classroom experience demonstrated that students' beliefs about themselves as mathematical thinkers and about their sense of belonging in a mathematical environment had profound influence on their performance in developmental courses. The results of the productive persistence interventions are striking, dramatically increasing the rate of student success in roughly half the time (American Association of Community Colleges, 2014; Yamada, 2014). As the number of faculty and campuses that adapt these interventions in their own local contexts grow, the results vary within a small range, while the impact of this best practice spreads to thousands of students in many states (Carnegie Foundation for the Advancement of Teaching, 2015).

The University of Missouri–Columbia went through a similar process of learning from others when senior leaders were charged with substantially increasing the student engagement of large numbers of first-year students without increasing costs. At a conference, one of the team members from Missouri attended an impressive presentation on assessment of nonresidential learning community outcomes at the University of Washington (UW). Members of a small group from academic and student affairs who were inspired by the presentation visited UW to learn first hand about the practices that produced these outcomes. Adapting elements of UW's program and other approaches found in the literature, they created a cross-functional team to design, implement, and assess first-year residential learning communities at Missouri. A pilot program with 240 students grew over a decade to involve more than 4,000 students annually. Ongoing assessments using unobtrusive measures (e.g., retention, GPA, graduation rates) coupled with national surveys such as NSSE provided persuasive evidence of the efficacy of the program and resulted in it becoming one of the institution's signature undergraduate initiatives, even though the original idea came from someplace else (Schroeder, 1999, 2013).

Cultivate an Ethos of Positive Restlessness

Improvement requires not only specific actions but also a certain orientation toward ourselves and our institutions. Although we need to act with resolve, we also need to remain humble—what scholars studying improvement refer to as the assumption that your ideas and practices are "possibly wrong and definitely incomplete" (Bryk et al., 2015, p. 163). Or, as one of the authors was told by a campus leader during a very positive accreditation visit, "We are pleased you think we are doing well. We want you to help us figure out how we can be even better."

Scholars studying diversity and disability have highlighted the importance of this self-critical attitude. Some institutions have taken a check-list approach to such work, establishing an office or program and then, in essence, ticking that topic off the college's to-do list. Shaun Harper's (2009) synthesis of research on Black male undergraduate student engagement reveals the perils of *not* being positively restless. Harper demonstrates that many individuals and institutions seem to see only the perceived deficits of Black male students, which leads to a particular "orientation (focus on stereotypical characteristics associated with the culture of disadvantage and poverty), discourse (lack of preparation, motivation, study skills, blaming students and/or their backgrounds), and strategies (compensatory educational programs, remedial courses, special programs, all focused on fixing the student)" (p. 148). Harper shows how this often prompts institutions to treat all Black males the same, ignoring what could be learned from the experiences of high achieving Black male undergraduates if campuses switched from expecting deficits to looking for assets.

Similarly, attention to architectural design for deafspace (Bauman, 2014; Edwards & Harold, 2014) by researchers and faculty at Gallaudet University, the world's only university designed for deaf and hard of hearing students, offers significant lessons about space, proximity, and contrast for anyone interested in creating classrooms and informal learning spaces that promote face-to-face community.

Within these deaf-friendly (and, indeed, hearing-friendly) spaces, class sessions often begin with a simple ritual of establishing visual connection before teaching begins. As students enter, the professor will establish eye contact with each, and students are encouraged to greet one another in a similar way. Bags, cups of coffee, and other visual distractions are removed, opening up the visual field to encourage direct connection. Then, throughout the class, eye contact is maintained as much as possible, facilitated by the design of the space and thoughtful choice of pedagogy.

> The student (and faculty) experience in such a classroom, sometimes called a "Sensory Commons" at Gallaudet, can feel dramatically different from what happens daily at other universities, as students may drift anonymously through classrooms and across campus. (Felten & Bauman, 2013, p. 374)

As the universal design movement has demonstrated, regularly questioning assumptions related to disability frameworks often yields positive insights with broad implications for all students, not just the ones labeled disabled (Burgstahler, 2015).

Successful programs and institutions often display this type of positive restlessness. In 2011, Purdue University launched a major initiative, Foundations of Excellence, to improve the experience of first-year students on campus. Although the institution's first- to second-year retention rate hit an all-time high that year at 90.6%, faculty and staff believed that more could and should be done. A 200-member task force spent a year working on this project, guided by high-level leadership including the vice provost for undergraduate affairs, the vice president for student affairs, the chief diversity officer, and the associate vice president for housing and food services. Task force recommendations yielded changes in the core curriculum, advising and student support services, faculty development, and other areas. The task force also established robust assessment processes to ensure that future improvements to the first year would be informed by evidence. Although the task force had completed its work, members recognized that their aspirations required continuing to look for ways to improve (Hamon, 2012).

Model the Process of Improvement for Students and the Institution

Paying attention to the processes that support improvement has two distinct benefits: (a) We can actually get better at getting better, and (b) we can model and teach students (and others) to learn how to think about and work on improvement in many aspects of their own lives.

The field of improvement science began with industry and medicine and recently has been adapted for education by the Carnegie Foundation for the Advancement of Teaching. This approach rests on a set of principles, three of which are particularly appropriate here:

- *Make the work problem specific and user centered:* Effective improvement efforts typically focus on concrete, clearly defined problems that are of concern to the people involved in the effort.

- *See the system that produces the current outcomes:* Whatever you are trying to improve exists within a context, and that context matters. By looking at both specific problems and the environment that produces and sustains those problems, you will be more apt to recognize both resources that can aid your improvement efforts and challenges that will need to be addressed.

· *Use inquiry to drive improvement:* Inquiry is a powerful tool for improvement, particularly at academic institutions where many people are trained and motivated by research. (Bryk et al., 2015, pp. 12–17).

Georgetown University is using a process like this as part of a strategic initiative called Designing the Future(s) of the University (Georgetown University, 2015). This project challenges the entire university community to invent new approaches to a distinctly Georgetown education, focusing in particular on enhancing the depth and quality of student learning while reducing or controlling costs. The experiments seeded by this initiative vary widely, challenging customs such as when, where, and how students earn credits toward a degree. To bring students into the heart of this endeavor, the Board of Regents Future(s) Fellows Program supports a cohort of 25 undergraduates working together with faculty and staff on sustained projects aimed at improving and reinventing the university.

By publicly modeling the improvement process and bringing students into the work, projects like this help the institution to get better and students (and others in the campus community) to develop the kinds of practical reasoning capacities that are essential to working and living in the modern world (Sullivan & Rosin, 2008).

Conclusion

Assessment is a vital tool for improvement, especially when it is used in ways that serve what matters most in the college experience. In an era of often intrusive external oversight, many on campus are suspicious—or just plain tired—of initiatives promising change. Yet, as Charles Schroeder recently concluded in *About Campus*, "If you don't have a sense of an improvement-oriented ethos, and some commitment to a culture of evidence, then regardless of what other activities you sponsor, you're probably not going to create the kind of self-perpetuating, performance-based learning organization you desire" (Schroeder & Shushok, 2015, p. 16).

In short, a personal orientation toward and an institutional culture of positive restlessness are necessary for us to fulfill our aspirations for our students and our communities. Developing these can be challenging in a time of constraints and cynicism, but a persistent focus on what matters most—and on the vital purposes of higher education for our students and our world—can help individuals and institutions to do the hard work necessary to make positive, lasting change.

Questions for Reflection

1. How would you describe your institution's culture of assessment and improvement? How much does accreditation drive your assessment work?

2. What examples can you identify of evidence-informed action at your institution? What lessons can you draw from those examples for your next improvement efforts?

3. How (and with whom) are you sharing, on and beyond your campus, both the processes and the results of your improvement efforts?

4. How can you involve more stakeholders, including students and faculty, in improvement initiatives on your campus?

5. How can you and your institution most effectively model the improvement process for students?

6. How do you and your institution support professional development to help people and groups be more capable of using assessment for improvement?

7. How are you and your institution replicating, celebrating, and rewarding successful improvement efforts?

7

LEADERSHIP MATTERS

As the longtime chaplain of Elon University, Richard McBride championed the role of spirituality and religious life on campus. McBride's vision led to a decade-long process of collaborative leadership that moved his institution toward a strategic goal of developing students as global citizens. Although the particulars of his story may not resonate at all colleges and universities, the broad themes illustrate why sustained, aspirational leadership matters in the undergraduate experience.

When the United Church of Christ (UCC) founded Elon in a small town in North Carolina in the nineteenth century, the institution had a distinctly Protestant culture and student body. More than a century later, the world, the college, and the students had transformed. By the late twentieth century, Elon had moved through a long and amicable process from an active to a historical affiliation with the UCC. Elon's undergraduates now came from across the country and the globe, and they grew up in families from many faith traditions. Yet, from its creation, Elon's mission emphasized "freedom of thought and liberty of conscience." What would it mean for a university with that purpose, existing at this place and in this time, to support the spiritual and religious development of a more diverse student body?

Inspired by McBride's writings about this question, alumna Edna Truitt Noiles and her husband, Doug, funded an endowment to create the Truitt Center for Religious and Spiritual Life, with the mission "to encourage students to explore their faith, and the faiths of others, and then to go into the world to lead lives of reconciliation." Soon after that gift, the university launched a new strategic plan, conceived jointly by faculty, staff, students, alumni, administrators, and trustees. A central pillar of the plan committed the university to broadening the institution's commitment to diversity and global engagement and included a major goal of constructing a multifaith center to extend and deepen Chaplain McBride's and the Truitt Center's vision. A few years later, McBride retired, but the work continued with the leadership of a new chaplain, Jan Fuller, and a widening network of faculty, staff, friends, and alumni. Elon developed a strategic partnership with the Interfaith Youth Core, aligning the university's work with other like-minded colleges and universities across the country and seeding a number of new student groups, including a Better Together interfaith living–learning community. Parents of Jewish and Roman Catholic students raised considerable funds to endow the Sklut Hillel Center and the Roman Catholic Newman Center. Trustees put their own personal gifts behind the construction of the Numen Lumen Pavilion, a beautiful multifaith facility in the heart of campus housing all 17 members of the Truitt Center staff and featuring a large sacred space that can be configured to support a variety of worship and spiritual activities of faith traditions from around the globe, from large numbers of Roman Catholics to a handful of Zen Buddhists—and where, sometimes, these traditions might bump into each other, in comfortable or uncomfortable ways, so that students and the community at large could learn from these intersections. Inspired by all of these developments, faculty created the Center for the Study of Religion, Culture, and Society to convene interdisciplinary dialogues and to support scholarship that informs knowledge and action.

Although many contributed to this rethinking of the place of religious and spiritual life on Elon's campus, the evolving initiative has remained rooted in the university's mission to prepare students to think and act as global citizens and in McBride's original contention that understanding world religions and spiritual traditions is central to citizenship in the twenty-first century. The founders' deep commitment to freedom of thought and liberty of conscience has also continued to animate this work, nurturing a campus community that respects and values each person's religious traditions or spiritual background (Felten, Barnett, & Fuller, 2014).

Reflecting on the example of Elon and other universities doing similar work, Eboo Patel, founder of the Interfaith Youth Corps, noted at a 2014 White House–sponsored gathering that leaders in higher education, unlike their peers in business and politics, have the capacity and the staying power to work on the fundamental challenges facing our nation and our planet. Collaborative acts of long-term leadership rarely make headlines, Patel concluded, but now more than ever colleges and universities must lead the way in addressing complex global problems and strengthening the fabric of civil society.

Leadership Matters: Action Principles

1. Lead through collaborative practices.
2. Articulate clear, aspirational goals linked to institutional mission and values.

3. Cultivate a culture that keeps students and learning at the center of decision-making.

4. Foster shared responsibility and leadership at all levels of the institution.

5. Make strategic choices and take informed risks.

6. Focus on dynamic, improvement-oriented planning, executing, and communicating.

Lead Through Collaborative Practices

The model of a single heroic figure does not fit with the kind of intentional leadership needed to foster a culture dedicated to student learning. To lead in higher education requires a focus on relationships and collaboration. Shared governance, complex organizational structures, and the premium on individual autonomy and critical dialogue, among other factors, mean that leadership in a college or university is, by definition, "a collective process" that at its core is "collaborative and empowering" (Morrill, 2007, pp. 7, 14). Leading at any level of a college or university, from heading up a student group or a faculty committee to chairing a department or serving as a trustee, can be particularly difficult in times when resources are limited and opinions are polarized, not only on campus but also throughout our society. Often, colleges and universities devolve into constituency politics, characterized by self-interest and a siege mentality that is detrimental to both student learning and institutional health (Pierce, 2014). William Bowen and Eugene Tobin, former presidents at Princeton University and Hamilton

CHAPTER 7: LEADERSHIP MATTERS   139

College, respectively, recently concluded after an analysis of leadership in higher education, "What is most needed on the part of all parties, including both faculty and administrators, is not just a willingness to reject 'we' versus 'they' thinking, but an eagerness to embrace good ideas generated by others" (Bowen & Tobin, 2015, p. 211).

LaGuardia Community College president Gail Mellow (2014) describes this kind of collaborative leadership as "creating a culture of engagement" that involves as many people as possible in a collective, generative process. When LaGuardia undertook massive organizational change to more seamlessly connect academic affairs and student life to better advise students, the leadership team received input from more than 400 faculty and 150 staff and supported 20 people to work together to research practices at other institutions. The new advising model at LaGuardia created teams of faculty and staff and a new dean, requiring the reclassification of 72 positions. Although this could have been a contentious and difficult process, it was carried out in such a way that, despite being in a unionized environment, no complaints were filed during this reorganization. Faculty, staff, and students valued both the engaging process and the new structure that emerged to meet an important institutional goal.

Collaborative engagement like that at LaGuardia cannot be mandated; instead, leaders cultivate it by creating opportunities for individuals and units to learn to work together toward common aims. At California State University Northridge, when a new president championed the goal of the university becoming a more learning-centered institution, faculty, staff, and administrators embraced the challenge. However, their initial energy often yielded frustration and sometimes sparked conflict:

> Although we were increasingly focused on student learning, collaborative partnerships were not yet the norm and were difficult to achieve. With good intentions but insufficient consultation, departments and divisions chased problems across traditional boundaries and imposed solutions that caused problems with other department's procedures. . . . Addressing complex goals such as exceeding predicted student retention for peer universities with our demographics required even finer levels of cooperation. (Koester, Hellenbrand, & Piper, 2008, p. 15)

The precise practices of collaborative leadership will vary across contexts, of course. These practices, however, often necessitate not only spanning organizational boundaries but also respectfully engaging different cultures and values within an institution. Elizabeth Blake (1996) calls "student affairs and academic affairs the yin and yang of the American undergraduate experience" (p. 4). These two groups approach students and learning (and each other!) from distinct and sometimes contradictory perspectives. On many campuses, the same can be said for the chief financial officer and the chief academic officer, or the board of trustees and the faculty, or athletics and academics, or students who do and do not participate in fraternities and sororities. Bridging these cultural divides requires leaders to cultivate trust among and within diverse groups. As Benjamin Dunlap (2014), president emeritus of Wofford College, observes,

> Especially if a college's best strategy lies in enhancing the learning experience it can offer, the real trick is to enable other people's visions—eliciting them, supporting them, and finding some ways to fund them. Once this approach is undertaken, it's surprising how many visionary ideas are compatible with each other. Even more important, it's astonishing how devotedly and energetically people will work for an institution when they are assured of this sort of trust and opportunity. Admittedly, this mode of leadership may at times involve acting more like a cheerleader than a generalissimo. But, it will always be the president's responsibility to keep all the visions directed towards a single, over-arching goal. And, as Mahatma Gandhi once so memorably put it, "There go my people—I must hurry and catch up with them … for I am their leader." I would call this leading by enabling.

Articulate Clear, Aspirational Goals Linked to Institutional Mission and Values

Leaders at institutions that have long-standing commitments to high-quality undergraduate education speak regularly about the values that undergird the educational program. At many colleges and universities, this begins with the centrality of the arts and sciences to provide students with a foundation of knowledge; to prepare them as critical thinkers, ethical citizens, creative problem solvers, and effective writers and communicators; and to inspire them to live lives of meaning and purpose. Many institutions are also guided by the value of making higher education as accessible as possible as a social good and the surest path to greater social and economic advancement. More recently, some have embraced the goal of efficiently and inexpensively developing student competency in certain professional and technical fields, or even in the liberal arts (Kelchen, 2015). These values, and others, are important and inspiring, but they may slip below the horizon for individuals and groups on campus if leaders from all levels of the institution do not regularly and publicly affirm them—and connect those statements to specific priorities and actions.

The University of Texas at El Paso (UTEP) has long championed educational access and excellence to students from its region and state. As national attention to science, technology, engineering, and mathematics (STEM) education increased in higher education in the 1990s, UTEP faculty and administrators led the way in articulating the importance of STEM education for Hispanic undergraduates since nearly 80% of its (now) 23,000 undergraduates identify as Hispanic. UTEP's president, Diana Natalicio, made STEM education a central theme of the institution's public face. Scores of faculty worked together to enhance pedagogy and to develop students as peer leaders. Between 2001 and 2010, UTEP more than doubled the number of STEM baccalaureate degrees awarded to its Hispanic students, making the university the nation's second largest producer of STEM undergraduate degrees awarded to

Hispanics (Dowd, Malcom, & Bensimon, 2009). UTEP's Peer Led Team Learning program, which focuses on fields including chemistry and mathematics, is particularly notable, with a 96% graduation rate for peer leaders and more than 40% of those students enrolling in graduate school (Flores, Becvar, Knaust, Lopez, & Tinajero, n.d.).

Occasionally, an institution of higher education will press the vision reset button and attempt full-scale institutional transformation. Christopher Newport University in Virginia did just that in 1996 when it appointed Paul Trible as president. "We rejected the notion of incremental progress," Trible (2014) explains. "We said we're in the business of dramatic transformation." The institution sharpened its focus on the undergraduate experience and the arts and sciences, eliminated professional programs not in keeping with that vision, increased the rigor of academic programs, and committed to a student-centered institutional culture. This focus yielded impressive results: The university's applicant pool grew by more than 500% between 1996 and 2006, and the average SAT score of incoming students increased by more than 200 points. For Trible and his colleagues, putting students at the center did not mean coddling them but rather making student learning the lens through which all institutional activity would be viewed.

Sometimes crises bring into sharp focus how campus behaviors are misaligned with institutional mission and values. When an off-campus party at Wake Forest University in North Carolina resulted in many students requiring medical attention for severe alcohol intoxication, administrators and faculty took bold actions aligned with the institution's tradition of academic excellence. The Student Life Committee undertook a study of the strength and stability of Greek life, and a separate university committee examined off-campus residential life. Many substantive changes emerged from this work including the creation of a three-year on-campus residency requirement of undergraduates, renovation and construction of new on-campus venues for social events and parties, expanded campus-wide programming for students, the hiring of a substance abuse prevention coordinator, and a host of reforms to strengthen Greek life on campus (Wake Forest University, 2010). Rather than turn away from the problem, Wake Forest leaders including President Nathan Hatch acknowledged the issue and addressed it by recommitting the university to high standards for the undergraduate experience.

One of the most demanding institutional contexts for collaborative leadership is when a college or university is undergoing substantive changes in institutional mission. This sometimes happens at private institutions, but it has become more common for public institutions as some Florida and Texas community colleges, for instance, are being legislatively transformed from two-year-degree-granting institutions into limited four-year-degree-granting state colleges. At the same time, a number of public baccalaureate-level institutions that historically offered only upper-division courses also have recently been legislatively mandated to begin offering the first two years of undergraduate education, such as Governor's State University (GSU) in Illinois. GSU is committed to making this transition without losing its mission of providing high-quality undergraduate education that is accessible to all students. As it prepared to admit its initial cohort of first-year students in 2014, GSU created affordable campus residences with live-in faculty mentors, a three-course learning community requirement for first-year students staffed entirely by full-time faculty, a systematic focus on writing in first- and second-year courses, and clear curricular pathways integrating general education and the majors. Executing these significant changes takes collaborative leadership engaging a broad cross section of institutional constituencies working together to enact the mission and values of the university.

A compelling vision for excellence in undergraduate education and a relentless focus on student learning—coupled with highly collaborative practices, intentional community engagement, involvement of manifold constituencies, and supporting the plans and visions of those aligned with the overarching vision—represent the most essential characteristics of a leadership strategy that can create a campus environment committed to student success.

Cultivate a Culture That Keeps Students and Learning at the Center of Decision Making

Campus cultures are like organisms that must be carefully tended to stay healthy and thrive. When the simple question, what is best for students and their learning? frames decision making at an institution, a reinforcing cycle develops to ensure that learning will be a central priority across campus. Indeed, inquiry is an essential leadership tool in the academy, and effective leaders at any level typically are more likely to pose critical questions than dictate what must happen (Marquardt,

2005). In their (2011) study on *Enhancing Campus Capacity for Leadership*, Adrianna Kezar and Jaime Lester emphasize the importance of higher education leaders acting in ways that are "educationally oriented and are grounded in the academic culture," such as engaging in intellectual discussions and partnering with students (p. 98).

Alverno College's story is perhaps the best-known example of the way questions and inquiry can enhance, even transform, both individual students and an institution. In the 1970s, Alverno struggled to survive as a small, Catholic women's college in Milwaukee, Wisconsin. After a discernment process that engaged faculty, staff, and students in questions about the purposes of the college, Alverno emerged with a fundamentally new curriculum based on eight core abilities and an assessment-as-learning culture. Students no longer earn conventional grades that measure their performance at the end of a course, but rather they continuously gather and reflect in a portfolio that documents their own learning. Students receive narrative feedback from faculty and also from working professionals and fellow students to help them reach ever-higher performance standards linked to each ability. Faculty also stepped out of traditional academic structures, becoming part of a matrix organization in which individual faculty members identify with both a disciplinary department (for example, psychology) and also an interdisciplinary group focused on one of the eight core abilities (for example, problem solving or valuing). Alverno students, faculty, and staff pioneered an assessment- and competency-based culture long before either had come into vogue (Hakel, 1997; Maki, 2010; Mentkowski & Associates, 2000).

Alverno might be seen as an outlier in higher education, yet a study by the American Association of State Colleges and Universities (AASCU) demonstrates that campus culture is essential at a wide variety of institutions. This AASCU study aimed to uncover why graduation rates varied so much among the organization's 420 member institutions. AASCU divided these 420 schools into 12 clusters of like institutions, and then sent research teams to the dozen top-performing institutions in each cluster to examine the programs, structures, and other factors that might explain why undergraduates at these colleges and universities graduated at such a higher rate (sometimes 50% more) than peers at institutions in the same cluster. George Mehaffy (2015), a vice president at AASCU, summarized the results succinctly: "What mattered most about graduation success was not a specific program or special funding but culture, a campus culture where faculty and staff believed that their role was to help students become successful" (p. 9).

Although single programs or leaders cannot create or sustain such a culture, individual actions can contribute to a campus ethos that values student learning. For instance, the Students as Learners and Teachers (SaLT) program offers all new faculty at Bryn Mawr and Haverford colleges, neighboring colleges in suburban Philadelphia, the opportunity to join in a weekly faculty seminar and semester-long partnerships with undergraduate student consultants. Participation is voluntary, but meaningful incentives supported by leaders at both institutions encourage all new faculty to take part. The most powerful part of SaLT is the student–faculty partnership; once each week a trained undergraduate consultant visits the faculty member's class to carefully observe a pedagogical issue the faculty member has identified (for example, patterns of student participation in seminar discussions or the ways students do, or do not, engage during lectures). The student consultant and faculty partner then meet to discuss these observations, drawing on both the disciplinary expertise faculty bring to the conversation and the insights consultants offer as peers of the students in the course. As the semester unfolds, both partners typically come to understand teaching and learning in new ways. Faculty participants often remark that their consultants helped them to rethink some of their classroom practices and to better understand the perspectives of students. Undergraduate consultants frequently echo the sentiments of one Bryn Mawr student: "Nothing is more powerful than seeing a professor take your ideas seriously, to have rich discussion about them and possibly see them implemented into a class. When I see a professor open to my ideas as a consultant, I feel that I am truly making a difference and becoming an important leader in this community" (Cook-Sather et al., 2014, p. 107). These partnerships upend the traditional assumption that an institution should be organized around how students learn from faculty and replace it with a more collaborative vision of leadership where all can learn from each other.

Campus cultures thrive when faculty, staff, and students see the creation of an extraordinary environment for learning as their common work. Campus goodwill is extended when ideas are honored from both the grass roots and the top of the organizational chart. Cooperation among campus constituencies becomes the norm in an environment of collaboration and transparency and when a genuine sense of community is honored. These characteristics of healthy campuses are fragile and should never be taken for granted. They need constant maintenance, cultivation, and public affirmation, and new members of campus communities must come to appreciate and respect their value. Ultimately, an important test of leadership at every level is to develop and cherish these elements of campus culture as a most precious institutional asset.

Foster Shared Responsibility and Leadership at All Levels of the Institution

Each constituency bears responsibility for the culture of leadership in an institution. (Elsewhere in the book we address faculty and staff extensively so we focus here on trustees, presidents, provosts, deans, students, and alumni.) Boards of trustees should have carefully thought-through succession plans to ensure continuity of strategic direction and policy formulation. Faculty senate leaders should be invited to join trustee meetings and senior staff retreats to encourage transparency and open dialogue. Collaboration across groups (faculty, students, staff, trustees, and others) in planning and visioning work can be a fruitful leadership experience for all. Presidents, provosts, vice presidents, and deans should continually be on the lookout for faculty, staff, and students who can be developed as institutional leaders. Elon University, for instance, hosts a faculty administrative fellows program that brings a tenured faculty member with an interest in administration to the senior staff table for a two-year fellowship, allowing her or him to tackle a challenging project and participate in day-to-day decision making at the senior level (Lambert, 2015). Bucknell

University in Pennsylvania has a successful executive intern program to pair student leaders with members of the senior staff of the university to assist with projects of institution-wide significance and help them develop as young leaders. Other key programs include department chair support and development, orientation for new trustees, alumni leadership programs, and comprehensive professional development for staff at all levels. In short, successful institutions intentionally cultivate leadership from within and do not simply rely on external hiring for new ideas and inspiration.

Harvard University professor Richard Chait, an expert on institutional governance and an adviser to many boards of trustees, is fond of quoting this old chestnut when advising governing boards: "The main thing is that the main thing *is* the main thing." In discharging their duties as key institutional leaders, trustees should examine every meeting agenda to ensure that the issues of (a) the quality of student learning and (b) the sufficiency of resources to support the vitality and centrality of the undergraduate experience are at the heart of their discussions.

It is very easy for boards to become otherwise distracted on peripheral issues or to become satisfied with a diet of presentations about solved issues delivered by the administrative team. Wise boards insist on clear institutional strategies, participate in campus planning processes side by side with other stakeholders, insist on measurable goals and outcomes, encourage appropriate levels of risk taking necessary to accomplish ambitious goals, and maintain the long view with regard to institutional culture and leadership succession planning in the senior ranks. Good boards also model generous philanthropy, committing personal wealth to support key priorities in undergraduate education. And, importantly, trustees need to continually interact with other campus leaders, regularly hearing from faculty, staff, and students directly about the nature and quality of the undergraduate experience (Keller, 2014).

Executive leadership is essential to an institutional focus on the quality of the undergraduate experience. Whether the president/chancellor plays the defining role in setting an institutional vision or focuses the creative work of many toward an overarching strategy, this role is undeniably important. A president must communicate a shared vision of a college or university's culture among faculty, trustees, alumni, students, parents, and other constituencies, all of whom see the institution from different vantage points. To keep all of these constituents on the same page, presidential communications must be frequent and consistent yet also personal (both one on one and in small and large groups) and tailored to special audiences (for example, columns in the alumni magazine and letters to parents).

To create lasting change in an institution's culture, years of focused work on key institutional priorities spanning a decade or more are often required. Unfortunately, the longevity of presidential administrations is often far shorter than that, which can result in a campus zigzagging from one vision and strategic plan to another in just a few short years, diminishing trust and creating institutional paralysis. Longer presidential tenure allows for relationships with many constituencies to be built over time, thus enabling greater buy-in about long-term goals and aspirations.

Provosts and chief academic officers (CAOs) also play a key role in shaping the learning environment, similar to the role of the president. CAOs are much more connected to the lives of faculty—the central and most important resource for students—and can play an instrumental role in fostering environments and initiatives that encourage faculty innovation, experimentation, and creativity. A provost plays a critical role in translating the broad vision for the institution into an action plan for the academic program, including all of the curricular and budgetary complexities involved. The provost also bears a great deal of responsibility for following through on the long-range planning process, ensuring that annual planning and budgeting are in concert with the broader strategic plan. For these reasons, strong, collaborative partnerships between CAOs and their respective chief financial officers are essential to institutional progress.

Effective provosts and CAOs also find ways to partner with their colleagues in student life to create institutional environments that help students foster connection between in- and out-of-classroom learning. Institutions that consistently focus on best practices in undergraduate education find effective strategies to bridge academic affairs and student life operations in a thoughtful and seamless manner.

Academic deans must be passionate advocates for their respective schools but at the same time connect the mission and aspirations of their units with the overall mission, culture, and strategic direction of the institution. Deans who think only about the welfare of their units can quickly create silos—powerful ones—that can become cultural forces working against the overall institutional mission. Differences about the value of teaching and student contact, the centrality of the arts and sciences to the overall curriculum, and resource control can lead to significant and intractable institutional tensions.

Student leadership also can be a positive force in campus culture. Student leadership is typically understood in terms of student government, clubs and organizations, as well as leadership development programs and minors and majors in leadership studies on some campuses. Those structures are important, but students also can act as grassroots leaders who profoundly shape the academic and social culture of a campus. For instance, in 2011, the student leaders at Duke University created an Intellectual Climate Committee to investigate the student experience inside and outside the classroom. These Duke undergraduates did this on their own because they were dissatisfied with the intellectual climate on campus—and they held themselves responsible for changing it (Spector, 2012). At about the same time, after a series of reports about distressing student behavior involving alcohol and sexual assault, Bucknell University's president, John Bravman, charged a special task force to research the situation and to offer specific advice about how to improve the student experience on campus. That group's first recommendation urged the president and the entire university to "engage, educate, and empower our students so that they can be key catalysts for improving the campus climate" (Bucknell University, 2011, p. 5).

Although students contribute to institutional culture in myriad ways, many institutions do not consider that alumni, too, can be active partners in shaping the campus learning environment. Yet at every institution, the lives and careers of successful alumni can be beacons to guide current students. Besides the inspiring examples they set, alumni can actively mentor current students and assist them with securing internships and employment. The Alumni Sharing Knowledge (ASK) program of DePaul University, for instance, taps 1,000 alumni mentors to help transition DePaul students to careers. Many alumni also enjoy opportunities to speak with current students through guest lecturing in classes and forming one-on-one mentor relationships. Finally, the Center for Assessment and Research Studies at James Madison University in Virginia coordinates an alumni survey on a five-year cycle that corresponds with each academic department's program review, giving faculty the opportunity to ask the department's graduates to give them information and feedback targeted to the specific program's goals and mission.

Make Strategic Choices and Take Informed Risks

Successful institutions must have sharply focused missions and carefully set priorities. If an institution is to be serious in asking the question about what matters most for a student's education, the answers to that powerful question will determine which long-term strategic goals the institution will pursue, which priorities will animate its fundraising, and how the institution will make a long-term commitment to those priorities in allocating resources. And let's be clear: If the resources are not committed to fund priorities, then they are not really priorities. Leadership is not about words alone or about jumping on the next higher education bandwagon. Leaders act. And leaders back up those actions with ongoing support, financial and otherwise.

Truly committing to excellence in any worthwhile endeavor involves confronting the possibility of failure. It takes courage for an institution to declare that it aspires to excellence in undergraduate education and to publicly set high, measurable standards for accountability. Even with broad-based support for a particular programmatic agenda, inevitably there will still be skepticism to overcome. Risk taking can also involve challenges such as suspending programs that are no longer central to the mission, or taking on a reasonable degree of debt to fund critical infrastructure, or setting ambitions high enough to push campus leaders out of their comfort zones. Risk taking will test the courage, perseverance, and resolve of campus leaders at all levels.

Both individuals and institutions assume risk in charting new paths. When Laura Gambino gave up a tenured faculty job to become a founding faculty member at Guttman Community College in New York City, many of her colleagues asked her how she could give up so much. Gambino replied, "How can I not take this opportunity? [We have] the chance to create a culture of learning and assessment for learning from the start of a new college" (Association of American Colleges and Universities, 2013). In the process of establishing this new institution, Guttman's faculty and staff took a number of significant but informed risks. Faculty teach in disciplines but are hired into the college as a whole, not in traditional academic departments. All students must attend full-time during their first year at Guttman so that they can be immersed in a highly structured and collaborative curricular and co-curricular program. Assessment drives decision making at all levels of the college through well-defined systems of gathering, analyzing, and acting on evidence of student learning. In these ways, and many more, Guttman's leaders are taking strategic risks to create a distinctly different model for community college education in the United States.

Leaders at Miami Dade College, a large multicampus community college in Florida, also took bold, calculated risks beginning in 2012 to improve student completion. First, the college formed a 27-member faculty task force to revise the curriculum, often one of the most contentious activities an institution can undertake. The committee was charged with mapping clear pathways for students through the major programs within the curriculum. Some faculty doubted whether such pathways were necessary until the committee attempted to simulate advising sessions with a number of students in different programs. While they were working on a particularly complex case involving a student in biology, one committee member, who had to that point been skeptical of the pathways initiative, joked, "I think I'll recommend that the student major in English, because I can figure that out" (quoted in Bailey, Jaggars, & Jenkins, 2015, p. 43). After the new pathways began to yield positive outcomes for students, leaders at the college noticed that assessment data suggested pathways were most effective when students met with professional advisers. The combination of a pathway and an adviser increased student persistence by nearly 10%. The college then invested $1 million to hire, train, and equip a corps of advisers. Evidence informed the decision making of college leaders throughout this process, but they still took considerable risks in political and financial capital to improve student outcomes.

For both Gambino and the leaders at Miami Dade College, the stakes were high, but they acted because the potential benefits aligned with their aspirational goals for the academy. Leaders throughout higher education, from staff to trustees, must do the same.

Focus on Dynamic, Improvement-Oriented Planning, Executing, and Communicating

So far in this chapter we have advanced the idea that leadership focused on the quality of the collegiate experience should be a collaborative enterprise that involves individuals and groups throughout an institution working together toward shared goals. In this final section, we focus on specific leadership tasks that are essential to shape a campus culture that is centered on the undergraduate experience.

The formulation of a long-term strategic plan is an important part of realizing an institution's vision. Planning processes afford institutions opportunities for all campus constituencies to have stakes in determining specifically how campuses will evolve over a 5-, 7-, or even 10-year time frame. Done well, strategic planning processes help center campuses on their top priorities for academic and programmatic investments, facilities, endowment objectives, and other hallmark initiatives aligned with the institution's vision. Good strategic plans are created for internally driven, purposeful, authentic reasons, not simply as bureaucratic exercises to meet external reporting requirements.

The chances that strategic plans will come to fruition are increased if some basic principles are followed. The first is to have long-term budgetary and resource allocation processes aligned with the plan's major goals. Multiyear budgets should be constructed for each goal, citing the specific source of revenues (e.g., operating, fundraised, endowment), simply because goals without associated resources are not likely to be realized. A 10-year strategic plan without an associated 10-year resource plan will be doomed to failure. At the same time, annual planning and budgeting processes must be aligned with the strategic plan. Many strategic goals are too costly and complex to be achieved in a single year. These larger goals can only be approached incrementally over a multiyear period, making an ambitious goal seem more attainable; this is especially true for institutions without massive wealth. (It is amazing what large-scale progress can be achieved over time when big goals are tackled with diligence and consistency, year by year! But this requires leadership to maintain discipline and focus.) When strategic planning guides annual goal setting and budgeting, there is also much less chance the strategic vision will be set aside in favor of the tyranny of the urgent.

Second, to ensure accountability, strategic plans should have measureable outcomes and avoid goals phrased as vague generalities. Campus constituents must be able to answer the question, "How will we know specifically when we have achieved these goals?" Strategic plans should be clearly summarized and communicated so that all campus constituencies, including faculty, alumni, parents, and other key parties, can be informed advocates for broad institutional aims. To increase the chances of a strategic plan actually being executed (and a large number never are!), a specific individual should be named on internal documents as the responsible party for shepherding each goal to completion.

Even though planning, budgeting, and execution are often on the top of administrative leaders' to-do lists, communication is also essential for collaborative colleges and universities focused on student learning. It is perhaps natural for complex organizations to become highly compartmentalized. Colleges and universities can all too easily resemble loose confederations of schools, departments, and administrative units, each struggling to maintain as much control of turf, budget, and curriculum as possible. If a unity of vision and intentionality of institution-wide focus on student learning is to be achieved, a key role of leadership at all levels is to communicate.

Higher education communication strategies often focus on presidential speeches, major publications about the student experience (for example, the prospective student viewbook), institutional websites, social media campaigns, and the like. While all of these are important, they provide no substitute for regular, in-person, relationship-building experiences that bring people together across institutional subgroups. Examples include

· Annual retreats with student government leaders and administrators to talk about matters of mutual interest
· Conversation groups of faculty, staff, and students on topics of institution-wide importance
· Regularly including faculty, staff, and students in board of trustee meetings and in social time with the board

· Discussion of white papers on matters of strategic importance across a range of institutional constituencies, including alumni, boards and councils, faculty, and staff

· Leadership summits (for example, for faculty leaders, parent leaders, alumni leaders) that help groups see the institution from a broader perspective, understand key goals, plans, and priorities and form relationships with other institutional leaders

These activities are designed to do much more than provide information. They help to lower the walls between institutional units and groups, to build trust, to promote understanding of how issues are seen from the vantage point of others, and to provide a basis for relationship building. Ultimately, institutions of higher learning are about the quality of relationships that exist on campus. Clear and transparent planning, budgeting, and communication practices are vital means to cultivate strong relationships within and beyond institutions.

Conclusion

Effective leadership at all levels of colleges and universities is essential to creating an institutional culture focused on what matters most in undergraduate education. Many of the key tenets in this regard are simple and straightforward: Work collaboratively; seek great ideas from all levels of the institution; have a well-thought-out, long-term strategic plan and execute it; and approach big institutional decisions through good questions about student learning.

While simple to state, these tenets are difficult to put into practice. They require the right set of institutional actors, a spirit of laser-like focus and intentionality, a willingness to persevere over many years to pursue complex and difficult institutional goals, a commitment to make choices and sacrifices, and institutional teamwork and cooperation. They also thrive best in an environment of trust. As Brian Rosenberg, president of Macalester College, in Minnesota, observes, "I think organizations with a culture of suspicion make decisions to avoid the worst, while those with a culture of trust make decisions to aspire to the best" (quoted in Bowen & Tobin, 2015, p. 212).

Questions for Reflection

1. How does your institution cultivate leadership at all levels? Do you have programs for engaging students, alumni, and others in leadership on campus?

2. How can you enhance shared responsibility for leadership at your institution?

3. What are some specific examples of ways that institutional values and priorities guide leadership and decision-making in your context?

4. When do you and other leaders on your campus take strategic risks? Who are the leaders on campus who are most

likely to take risks? What have you and your colleagues learned from these experiences with risk taking?

5. Does your program and campus have a strategic planning and resource allocation process in place that is linked to your campus vision of what matters most for student learning and success?

6. How does your institution determine its highest priorities? How does learning factor into these priorities?

8

ACTING ON WHAT MATTERS MOST

As we said from the outset, our aim has been to write a brief, useful book that helps you and your colleagues develop the shared vision, focused will, and nimble skills necessary to do the transformational work of higher education. We believe that a necessary step in that process is to ask two important questions: What matters most in the undergraduate experience? What is possible when institutions focus on what matters most?

By concentrating on these questions, researching the scholarly literature, and investigating a wide range of practices and programs at colleges and universities, we identified a set of six common themes we believe are at the heart of what matters most in the undergraduate experience. Although colleges and universities differ in many important ways, all excellent undergraduate education has these characteristics at its core.

We recognize that diverse institutions have varying assets and face distinct challenges. One size does not fit all in higher education, nor will a single tool or approach work equally well in every context. Our framework is meant to be practical and helpful, not perfect or comprehensive. However, we firmly believe that by focusing on what matters most in your individual context, and by critically analyzing examples of what works at other colleges and universities, you will find the best strategies for your students and your institution.

This set of themes, and the book as a whole, is meant to act as a heuristic for you as you reflect on your institution, on its goals and programs, and how it could most effectively deliver on what matters most. We hope you will find the Action Principles and Questions at the end of each chapter (and collectively in Appendix A and Appendix B) useful tools for stimulating critical reflection and discussion. We will briefly restate the themes here, not simply to repeat them but to serve as a reminder for you to *use* them.

What Matters Most

Learning Matters
Student learning is at the heart of undergraduate education. Focusing on learning—for students, faculty, staff, administrators—is the central work of effective colleges and universities. The promotion of learning at all levels and in many ways must be the dominant and guiding criterion for as many institutional decisions as possible.

Relationships Matter
Student-faculty, student-staff, and student-student relationships account in very large measure for the powerful learning that undergraduates experience. For a college or university to sustain excellence, other structural relationships also matter a great deal, such as those between academic affairs and student affairs on campus, between the governing board and senior administrators, and between alumni and their

alma mater. Strong institutions cultivate and nurture environments where healthy relationships form and flourish.

Expectations Matter

Clear and high expectations are central to encouraging and challenging students to stretch themselves to grow and excel both in and beyond the classroom. Effective institutions communicate expectations clearly and consistently, and ensure that programs and practices enact these expectations, so that everyone from prospective and enrolled students to staff and faculty understand and experience what matters most.

Alignment Matters

Institutional effectiveness and success are enhanced when administrative and academic policies, procedures, and processes are aligned in an integrated and seamless fashion. This alignment is improved through educational partnerships within and across traditional organizational boundaries, especially academic and student affairs units. When students find themselves in an aligned institution, their experiences are more connected, coherent, and meaningful.

Improvement Matters

Some institutions not only expect students to learn and improve, but they model an improvement ethos for students by aspiring for higher levels of accomplishment and by staying true to their purposes. These institutions seek out best practices and adapt research-based ideas to fit their own students, missions, and institutional cultures. They also engage in authentic assessment practices grounded in the everyday experience of students, faculty, and staff and use evidence to inform and improve everything they do.

Leadership Matters

At an effective institution, leadership is collaborative, and people throughout the institution see themselves as part of the leadership team. This entails articulating clear, aspirational goals and sustaining a culture that fosters shared responsibility and leadership at all levels of the institution.

Focus on Institutional Culture

We believe that no matter the circumstances, these six themes stand the test of time and are needed now more than ever as the central focus of undergraduate education. It is our hope you will reflect on these themes in your own context and then take meaningful action to enhance what matters most at your institution.

Focusing on the undergraduate experience is all about creating and sustaining an institutional culture that is mission-driven yet adaptable to change. Successful institutions have leadership at every level—students, faculty and staff, departments and divisions, schools and colleges, upper administration, the governing board—that is committed to putting student learning first. Such institutions also have a culture of positive restlessness (Kuh et al., 2010)—always assuming that they can do better, continually seeking improvement, and resisting the complacency and ossification that results from the "we've always done it this way" mindset.

We believe in the fundamental idea that institutional change is possible through strategic planning and then deliberate execution of those plans. Institutional cultures focused on student learning are fostered by a careful alignment of plans for program development and enhancement, new and renovated facilities, faculty development and support, fundraising objectives, and a host of priorities related to campus climate and the student experience. We recognize that both changing environments and sudden crises can make sustained action difficult; acts of violence or hatred, widespread student protests, sharp budget cuts, and other traumatic events can shake an institution to the core. A college or university is best able to weather these storms when leaders at all levels have a shared understanding of mission, a strong network of relationships stretching across and beyond campus, a habit of collaboratively working together to solve problems, and the ability to cultivate high levels of trust, including trust that commitments made today will be honored in the future.

Planning begins with an authentic vision and a clear sense of mission. Institutions must involve multiple constituencies in the development of strategic plans by cultivating the distinct expertise and perspectives of each. Many colleges and universities have established ways of engaging their boards of trustees in setting long-term visions, but savvy institutions also integrate faculty, staff, and students into this work. Leaders of the most effective strategic planning efforts reach beyond the traditional academic constituencies to make alumni, families, employers, foundations, and government agencies partners in the process.

In short, our long experience tells us that collaborative planning is an essential tool to developing and sustaining institutional culture focused on learning.

Having a strong strategic plan is one thing, but enacting it is another. We have seen too many strategic plans filed and forgotten. Long-term planning that leads to systemic change must be linked to annual priority setting, budgeting and hiring, and other key institutional functions. And we cannot overemphasize the need for frequent communication about strategic initiatives so that all constituents are informed about progress and reminded about the broad goals and principles undergirding these efforts. Celebrating milestones and accomplishments along the way also nourishes an institution's spirit and morale. At the same time, publicly acknowledging the persistent challenges on our campuses ensures that we continue to work toward aspirational goals.

The creation of an institutional culture focused on student learning can be stymied by common pitfalls related to a lack of broad involvement and poor communication. Try to avoid these! Our first and most important recommendation in this regard is to involve a broad range of people in thinking about how the institution might focus more fully on issues of student learning and to welcome ideas from all over campus. Leaving out a key constituency can encourage resentment and feelings of alienation and will usually slow progress. To encourage the most robust dialogue possible, give all participants in the conversation the freedom to speak their piece. It is essential that trustees hear directly from faculty and staff (and vice versa) and that student voices are listened to with care. A climate in which honest exchange is not possible will likely lead to less than optimal outcomes. It is also essential that serious conversations about student learning not be derailed by conversation stoppers such as "We tried that once before and it failed" or "So and so would never agree to that." Good ideas should be given the time and support necessary to develop. Over and over again we have seen institutions do hard but important work to enhance student learning, finding the will and the money to do what they most want to do. The central question is, what do you most want to do?

Creating an institutional culture focused on student learning is a long-term game. There are no quick fixes. It is fashionable in the academy to look for best practices that show immediate results on key metrics. Some interventions have been demonstrated empirically to have positive influence on student success, but not all of these may be applicable to every institution in the same way. On the journey toward excellence, there is no single path. Institutional contexts are hugely determinative of what works. You need to consider the intersections between your context and possible practices to find the best approaches for your students and your institution, and you need to be open to changing your practices over time as your students and your situation evolve.

Despite the complexity of this work, every institution can make a conscious choice to reach a higher level of excellence, no matter what its starting point. Yes, institutional resources and degrees of wealth vary and can make all kinds of things possible, or seemingly impossible. Nevertheless, we believe that all institutions can attain their specific missions through effective educational practices that are most appropriate for the students they serve. Marshal your best thinkers, planners, communicators, and advocates for excellence, and improve or redesign the institution so that it will best serve the students you are privileged to have.

It is our firm conviction that institutions that are serious about creating learning-centered cultures have to constantly make strategic choices that reflect their values. These choices are revealed by the content of meetings of faculty, senior leaders, and boards of trustees. They are evident in budget priorities. They emerge in fundraising campaigns. And they are apparent in the ways classes are designed and taught; the daily interactions students have with faculty, staff and peers, and in the ethos of a campus.

We believe that aspects of the institutional culture itself must be the subject of regular, critical study. Routine gatherings of trustees, the faculty, or senior administrators seldom examine broad questions of institutional culture, and this inattention can lead to cultural drift or to the neglect of essential issues, such as sexual violence or race relations on campus. A seemingly stable environment can be shattered almost overnight if a college or university strays carelessly from its mission by not paying attention to how historic inequities or recent developments in the broader society are affecting campus life, by focusing the reward system on the wrong priorities, or by experiencing rapid turnover in leadership. Rather than waiting for a crisis to arise, prudent leaders should notice what is *not* being talked about and should seek to bring hard truths into the open, perhaps through the appointment of institutional task forces charged with the examination of some dimension of campus life. In our experience, a strong, positive, campus culture focused on learning is an enormous asset that should never be taken for granted.

Make Learning Central

We have observed that many institutions begin to get serious about improving the student experience after facing decreases in student enrollment and retention. And we are realists; we know that retention matters. We know that this particular metric influences fiscal survival, institutional reputation within a state or region, and status in national rankings, including in *US News & World Report.*

It is disheartening and an unwise use of the scarce societal resources devoted to higher education to see a significant percentage of students—even a majority—leave institutions only to be replaced by others who will enter through the same revolving door and, once again, not meet with success. And we know that we cannot improve our country's record on affording equal educational opportunity until we improve our retention and graduation rates for historically underserved students. But we should remember that students come to college not simply to be retained but also to attain their goals to build meaningful lives and careers. Therefore, we strongly believe that focusing on retention as a primary metric is an insufficient aspiration. Retention can be more accurately viewed as a by-product of what matters much more—student learning and success. Institutions must begin by finding better ways of describing what effective student learning looks like and connecting these visions to structural change and improved practices, procedures, and processes. Retention rates will follow. Our thinking and language need to be altered; retention as an end in itself shortchanges the student experience.

One dimension of making learning central to campuses that deserves much greater attention is helping students integrate their various learning experiences. Excellent undergraduate education prompts students to make connections between classroom and out-of-classroom learning, between college and career, and between academic disciplines and personal purpose. All too often, we fear, this is left to happenstance. Some students have meaningful pull-it-all-together experiences during internships or senior capstone courses or through writing essays for graduate school or international fellowships such as the Fulbright or the Rhodes. But it is not enough to hope that students have synthesizing experiences during their final years. Institutions should not leave integration to chance, hoping units and people across campus will coordinate on their own. Nor should colleges and universities trust that a few key people or programs can foster integration for all students. Instead institutions must intentionally integrate their own curricula and programs to make this kind of student experience possible for all students. Colleges and universities should transform silos into systems by supporting cross-institution cooperation and by paying more attention to how students experience their institutions than the formalities of organizational charts.

To learn and develop in optimal environments, students need to be immersed and mentored in high-impact learning practices. We urge you to remember the importance of making such experiences available for *all* students, not just for the best students or students who can afford them. For example, internships (particularly unpaid ones) and summer undergraduate research experiences can result in additional expenses for students and families that may put these programs out of reach for students who are counting on jobs to help cover upcoming tuition bills. In a similar vein, study abroad and domestic study away programs often result in both additional expenses and lost opportunities to work for pay. Careful budgeting and creative planning can address some of these concerns. At the same time, endowments and annual fund gifts from alumni and parents can dramatically increase accessibility and are easy asks for fundraising because many people have witnessed the power of these learning experiences and want others to have similar opportunities.

Another important but sometimes overlooked dimension of learning is the influence of students on other students. Although faculty and staff, high-impact practices, and the myriad programs that institutions put into place to enhance the student experience are essential, researchers are clear that the greatest influences on students during the undergraduate years are other students (Astin, 1993; Pascarella & Terenzini, 2005). We must pay greater attention to how we can most effectively encourage and structure the kinds of student interaction that will enhance learning.

Partnering with students in exploring the question of peer influences is an obvious starting point. Students are an essential and too often ignored asset for institutional planning and assessment. They have many good ideas to offer through their lived experience, and their perceptions of their needs and preferences can profoundly influence the outcome of any planning activity. Students who are partners in this kind of work while on campus will be, in the future, the engaged alumni who will serve the college or university for the long term.

As with students, institutions too often miss opportunities to engage the leadership of their boards in envisioning institutions that are truly learning focused. An effective board supports and encourages quality throughout the institution, expects measurable outcomes, keeps a sharp eye on bold ideas, advocates for resources to support learning (and trustees often give generously with their own personal resources), encourages calculated risk taking, establishes and renews a strategic vision for the institution, and demonstrates courage in taking on the most ambitious institutional goals. Trustees can and should be champions for learning.

Finally, we conclude this section by reemphasizing that an essential element of an institutional culture focused on student learning is the unrelenting commitment to collaboration across organizational lines. Institutional change can occur at a more rapid pace when all constituencies are rowing in the same direction. One key to collaboration is to recognize and honor the fact that good ideas to improve student learning come from all levels of the institution—from grassroots faculty and staff conversations to the highest levels of administration—and that effective institutions find ways to refine, nurture, and support these ideas to turn them into constructive realities.

Take Action! Do Not Allow Constraints to Stymie Change

It is all too easy to dismiss working for positive change for one or more of the following reasons:

· Declining state support for higher education
· Lack of visionary or consistent leadership

· A scarcity of discretionary resources

· Inappropriate or outdated facilities

· No clear plan for the future

· Metrics and mandates that restrict flexibility

· Comfort with the status quo

· Not wanting to give in to the suggestions of critics or the demands of protesters

· A siloed and uncollaborative institutional culture

Even if all of these circumstances exist on your campus, our advice is not to get bogged down by these but to get the ball rolling right away. Small, sustained actions often build momentum. First, you must begin.

Focus on what you can control, even if that seems a small piece of the larger puzzle. As we have demonstrated throughout this book, deliberate and persistent work in individual courses or at department or program levels can yield significant outcomes for students and institutions. In addition, each of you has friends, colleagues, and supervisors whom you can cultivate through intentional interactions, deepening your work by developing your sphere of influence. One person frequently does make a difference. We have often seen small successes started by one individual snowball into systemic changes.

As you do this work, resources likely will be scarce. Of course money matters a great deal, but it isn't everything. Individuals and programs without big budgets and institutions without large endowments should use limited resources strategically in support of long-term goals. Programmatic targets for investment should be chosen wisely, whether supported by institutional annual budgets or endowment. Taking the optimistic view, we contend that a scarcity of resources requires individuals and institutions to be more imaginative, strategic, focused, and creative. Primacy should be given to programs that have the highest impact and value for students. Continued investments in key programs over the long term should be made to accomplish both transformational change and sustained excellence. You might be surprised how modest resources directed to a priority year by year over the course of a decade can result in a signature, high-quality point of pride for an entire institution. Focused attention on good ideas over the long term, coupled with appropriate investments, is almost always a winning formula.

An Optimistic Final Note

We care about improving colleges and universities—public and private, two-year and four-year—because we believe that higher education still affords the single greatest opportunity for both individual advancement and civic development in our society. Our optimism is fueled by hundreds of examples of thriving programs and institutions that are models of excellence in the undergraduate experience. A close examination of these success stories underscores our six core themes about what matters most.

Yet great challenges remain. Too many students do not succeed, leaving higher education before completing their degrees. Others enter our institutions and flounder, sometimes not finding the mentoring and support to help them discover their paths forward. Still others take five, six, or even more years to earn four-year degrees and equally prolonged periods to complete associate degrees. Some receive diplomas but are not fully pre-pared to enter the workforce or to live as citizens in a diverse world. These problems represent missed opportunities for too many individuals and also an inefficient use of personal, gov-ernmental, and philanthropic resources that we can ill afford to waste.

At the beginning of this volume we asked you to think about your own visions of what matters most and what you could do to make your institution a place where more students thrive and take the fullest advantage of their undergraduate experience. We hope you end this book inspired to turn your vision into a real-ity. Our students and our world need what higher education, and you, have to offer.

REFERENCES

Ambrose, S. A., Bridges, M. W., DiPietro, M., Lovett, M. C., & Norman, M. K. (2010). *How Learning Works: Seven Research-Based Principles for Smart Teaching*. San Francisco, CA: Jossey-Bass.

American Association of Community Colleges. (2014). *Empowering Community Colleges To Build the Nation's Future: An Implementation Guide*. Washington, DC: American Association of Community Colleges.

American College Personnel Association. (1994). *The Student Learning Imperative: Implications for Student Affairs*. Alexandria, VA: American College Personnel Association.

Anderson, P., Anson, C. M., Gonyea, R. M., & Paine, C. (2015). The Contributions of Writing to Learning and Development: Results from a Large-Scale Multi-institutional Study. *Research in the Teaching of English, 50*(2), 199–235.

Arcario, P., Eynon, B., Klages, M., & Polnariev, B. A. (2013). Closing the Loop: How We Better Serve Our Students Through a Comprehensive Assessment Process. *Metropolitan Universities Journal, 24*(2), 21–37.

Arum, R., & Roksa, J. (2011). *Academically Adrift: Limited Learning on College Campuses.* Chicago, IL: University of Chicago Press.

Arum, R., & Roksa, J. (2014). *Aspiring Adults Adrift: Tentative Transitions of College Graduates.* Chicago, IL: University of Chicago Press.

ASAP: Accelerated Study in Associate Programs (2015). Significant Increases in Associate Degree Graduation Rates: CUNY Accelerated Study in Associate Programs (ASAP). New York: The City University of New York. Retrieved on February 4, 2016 from   http://www1.cuny.edu/sites/asap/wp-content/uploads/sites/8/media-assets/ASAP-Program-Overview_121415.pdf

Association of American Colleges and Universities. (2013). *Assessment for Learning: Building a New Curriculum at Charles and Stella Guttman Community College.* Retrieved on May 20, 2014 from https://www.aacu.org/campus-model/assessment-learning-building-new-curriculum-charles-and-stella-guttman-community

Astin, A. W. (1984). Student Involvement: A Developmental Theory for Higher Education. *Journal of College Student Personnel, 25*, 297–308.

Astin, A. W. (1985). *Achieving Educational Excellence: A Critical Assessment of Priorities and Practices in Higher Education.* San Francisco, CA: Jossey-Bass.

Astin, A. W. (1993). Diversity and Multiculturalism on Campus: How Are Students Affected? *Change, 25*(2), 44–49.

Astin, A. W. (1993). *What Matters Most in College.* San Francisco, CA: Jossey-Bass.

Bailey, T. R., Jaggars, S. S., & Jenkins, D. (2015). *Redesigning America's Community Colleges: A Clearer Path to Student Success*. Cambridge, MA: Harvard University Press.

Baker, G. R. (2012). North Carolina A&T State University: A Culture of Inquiry. *NILOA Examples of Good Assessment Practice*. Urbana, IL: University of Illinois and Indiana University, National Institute for Learning Outcomes Assessment. Retrieved on March 17, 2013 from http://www.learning outcomeassessment.org/CaseStudy/NCAT.html

Banta, T. W., & Blaich, C. (2010). Closing the Assessment Loop. *Change, 43*(1), 22–27.

Barber, J. P. (2012). Integration of Learning: A Grounded Theory Analysis of College Students' Learning. *American Education Research Journal, 49*(3), 590–617.

Barefoot, B. O., Griffin, B. Q., & Koch, K. K. (2012). *Enhancing Student Success and Retention throughout Undergraduate Education: A National Survey*. Brevard, NC: John N. Gardner Institute for Excellence in Undergraduate Education. Retrieved December 17, 2014 from http://www.jngi.org/wordpress/wpcontent/uploads/2012/04/JNGInational_survey_web.pdf

Barr, R. B., & Tagg, J. (1995). From Teaching to Learning: A New Paradigm for Undergraduate Education. *Change, 27*(6), 12–25.

Barth, J., & Gess, P. (2015). *The Hendrix College Odyssey Program as Case Study: Context and Process*. AAC&U Annual Meeting, January 22, Washington, DC.

Bass, R. (2012). Disrupting Ourselves: The Problem of Learning in Higher Education. *EDUCAUSE Review* (March/April), 23–33.

Baum, S., & Ma, J. (2014). *Trends in College Pricing*. Princeton NJ: College Board.

Bauman, H. (2014). DeafSpace: An Architecture Toward a More Livable and Sustainable World. In H.-.D. L. Bauman & J. J. Murray (Eds.), *Deaf Gain: Raising the Stakes for Human Diversity*, 375–401. Minneapolis. MN: University of Minnesota Press.

Beld, J. M. (2010). Engaging Departments in Assessing Student Learning: Overcoming Common Obstacles. *Peer Review*, *12*(1), 6–9.

Benjamin, M. (Ed.). (2015). *Learning Communities from Start to Finish: New Directions for Student Services*, No. 149. San Francisco, CA: Jossey-Bass.

Bergquist, W. H., & Pawlak, K. (2007). *Engaging the Six Cultures of the Academy*. San Francisco, CA: Jossey-Bass.

Berrett, D. (2015, September 21). The Unwritten Rules of College. *Chronicle of Higher Education*. Retrieved September 22, 2015 from http://chronicle.com/article/The-Unwritten-Rules-of/233245/?key=Sz8lIwNvNS1FMXBqazkWMTpcYX NuOUgma3BJbC4iblFWGQ==#comments-anchor

Biggs, J., & Tang, C. (2011). *Teaching for Quality Learning at University*, (4th ed.). New York, NY: McGraw Hill.

Blaich, C., & Wise, K. (2011). *From Gathering to Using Assessment Results: Lessons from the Wabash National Study*, Occasional Paper #8. Urbana, IL: University of Illinois and Indiana University, National Institute for Learning Outcomes Assessment.

Blaich, C., & Wise, K. (2015). Knowing About vs. Knowing How. *Practitioners' Corner*. Crawfordsville, IN: Center of Inquiry at Wabash College. Retrieved on June 23, 2015 from www.centerofinquiry.org/practitioners-corner

Blake, E. S. (1996). The Yin and Yang of Student Learning in College. *About Campus*, 4–9.

Blimling, G., & Whitt, E. J. (1999). *Good Practice in Student Affairs: Principles to Foster Student Learning*. San Francisco, CA: Jossey-Bass.

Blumenstyk, G. (2015). *American Higher Education in Crisis? What Everyone Needs to Know*. New York, NY: Oxford University Press.

Bok, D. (2006). *Our Underachieving Colleges: A Candid Look at How Much Students Learn and Why They Should Be Learning More*. Princeton, NJ: Princeton University Press.

Botstein, L. (2005). The Curriculum and College Life: Confronting Unfulfilled Promises. In R. H. Hersh & J. Merrow (Eds.), *Declining by Degrees: Higher Education at Risk* (pp. 209–227). New York, NY: Palgrave Macmillan.

Bowen, W. G. (2013). *Higher Education in the Digital Age*. Princeton, NJ: Princeton University Press.

Bowen, W. G., & Levin, S. A. (2003). *Reclaiming the Game: College Sports and Educational Values*. Princeton, NJ: Princeton University Press.

Bowen, W. G., & Tobin, E. M. (2015). *Locus of Authority: The Evolution of Faculty Roles in the Governance of Higher Education*. Princeton, NJ: Princeton University Press.

Braxton, J. M., Vesper, N., & Hossler, D. (1995). Expectations for College and Student Persistence. *Research in Higher Education, 36*(5), 595–611.

Brownell, J. E., & Swaner, L. E. (2010). *Five High-Impact Practices: Research on Learning Outcomes, Completion, and Quality.* Washington, DC: American Association of Colleges and Universities.

Bruff, D. (2009). *Teaching with Classroom Response Systems: Creating Active Learning Environments.* San Francisco, CA: Jossey-Bass.

Bryant, J. (2014). *National Student Satisfaction and Priorities Report.* Coralville, IA: Noel-Levitz.

Bryk, A. S., Gomez, L. M., Grunow, A., & LeMahieu, P. G. (2015). *Learning to Improve: How America's Schools Can Get Better at Getting Better.* Cambridge, MA: Harvard Education Press.

Bucknell University. (2011). The Campus Climate for Bucknell University Students: A Multifaceted Analysis. President's Task Force on Campus Climate. Retrieved April 7, 2015 from http://ericriess.com/wp-content/uploads/.../BucknellCampus Climate2011.pdf

Burgstahler, S. E. (2015). *Universal Design in Higher Education* (2nd ed.). Cambridge, MA: Harvard Education Press.

Buskist, W., & Groccia, J. E. (Eds.). (2012). *Evidence-Based Teaching: New Directions for Teaching and Learning*, No. 128. San Francisco, CA: Jossey-Bass.

Busteed, B. (2014, December 1). The Real Disruptive Innovation in Higher Education. *Business Journal*, Retrieved December 17, 2014 from http://www.gallup.com/businessjournal/179564/real-disruptive-innovation-education.aspx

Cain, T. R., & Hutchings, P. (2015). Faculty and Students: Assessment at the Intersection of Teaching and Learning. In G. D. Kuh, S. O. Ikenberry, N. A. Jankowski, T. R. Cain, P. T. Ewell, P. Hutchings, & J. Kinzie (Eds.), *Using Evidence of Student Learning to Improve Higher Education* (pp. 95–116). San Francisco, CA: Jossey-Bass.

Cameron, W. B. (1963). *Informal Sociology: A Casual Introduction to Sociological Thinking*. New York, NY: Random House.

Carey, K. (2015). *The End of College: Creating the Future of Learning and the University of Everywhere*. New York, NY: Riverhead Books.

Carnegie Foundation for the Advancement of Teaching. (2015). Productive Persistence. Retrieved June 24, 2015 from http://www.carnegiefoundation.org/in-action/pathways-improvement-communities/productive-persistence/

Carnes, M. C. (2014). *Minds on Fire: How Role-Immersion Games Transform College*. Cambridge, MA: Harvard University Press.

Chambliss, D. F., & Takacs, C. G. (2014). *How College Works*. Cambridge, MA: Harvard University Press.

Chang, M. J., Denson, N., Saenz, V., & Misa, K. (2006). The Educational Benefits of Sustaining Cross-Racial Interaction

Among Undergraduates. *Journal of Higher Education, 77*(3), 430–455.

Chickering, A. W., & Gamson, Z. F. (1987). Seven Principles for Good Practice in Undergraduate Education. *AAHE Bulletin*, 3–7.

Chieffo, L., & Griffiths, L. (2004). Large-Scale Assessment of Student Attitudes After a Short-Term Study Abroad Program. *Interdisciplinary Journal of Study Abroad, 10*(4), 165–177.

Christopher Newport University. (2015). Center for Academic Success. Retrieved on November 30, 2015, from http://cnu.edu/academicsuccess/index.asp

Christopher Newport University. (2015). Faculty Resources. *College of Arts and Humanities.* Retrieved April 15, 2015 from http://cnu.edu/artsandhumanities/facultyresources/

Clydesdale, T. (2008). *The First Year Out: Understanding American Teens After High School.* Chicago, IL: University of Chicago Press.

Clydesdale, T. (2015). *The Purposeful Graduate: Why Colleges Must Talk to Students about Vocation.* Chicago, IL: University of Chicago Press.

Cole, D. (2008). Constructive criticism: The Role of Student–Faculty Interactions on African American and Hispanic Students' Educational Gains. *Journal of College Student Development, 49*(6), 587–605.

Cook-Sather, A., Bovill, C., & Felten, P. (2014). *Engaging Students as Partners in Learning and Teaching: A Guide for Faculty.* San Francisco, CA: Jossey-Bass.

Covington, M. V. (1992). *Making the Grade: A Self-Worth Perspective on Motivation and School Reform.* New York, NY: Cambridge University Press.

David, D. (2013). *California State University Foundation "Give Students a Compass": Interim Grant Progress Report to Walter S. Johnson Foundation.* Retrieved December 17, 2014 from http://www.calstate.edu/app/compass/february2013report .shtml

Deakin Crick, R. (2014). Learning to Learn: A Complex Systems Perspective. In R. D. Crick, C. Stringher, & K. Ren (Eds.), *Learning to Learn: International Perspectives from Theory and Practice* (pp. 66–86). New York, NY: Routledge.

Delbanco, A. (2012). *College: What It Was, Is, and Should Be.* Princeton, NJ: Princeton University Press.

Deresiewicz, W. (2014). *Excellent Sheep: The Miseducation of the American Elite and the Way to a Meaningful Life.* New York, NY: Free Press.

Dewey, J. (1910). *How We Think.* Lexington, MA: D.C. Heath.

Dowd, A. C., Malcom, L. E., & Bensimon, E. M. (2009). *Benchmarking the Success of Latino and Latina Students in STEM to Achieve National Graduation Goals.* Los Angeles, CA: University of Southern California.

Drake, J. K., Jordan, P., & Miller, M. A. (Eds.). (2013). *Academic Advising Approaches: Strategies That Teach Students to Make the Most of College.* San Francisco, CA: Jossey-Bass.

Drane, D., Micari, M., & Light, G. (2014). Students as Teachers: Effectiveness of a Peer-Led STEM Learning Program over 10 Years. *Educational Research and Evaluation, 20*(3), 210–230.

Dunlap, B. (2014). Personal correspondence with Leo Lambert. December 2014.

Dunne, E., & Zandstra, R. (2011). *Students as Change Agents: New Ways of Engaging with Learning and Teaching in Higher Education.* Bristol, UK: ESCalate HEA Subject Centre for Education, University of Bristol.

Dweck, C. (2006). *Mindset: The New Psychology of Success.* New York, NY: Ballantine.

Edwards, C., & Harold, G. (2014). DeafSpace and the Principles of University Design. *Disability and Rehabilitation, 36*(16), 1350–1359.

Ewell, P. T., & Jankowski, N. A. (2015). Accreditation as Opportunity: Serving Two Purposes with Assessment. In G. D. Kuh, S. O. Ikenberry, N. A. Jankowski, T. R. Cain, P. T. Ewell, P. Hutchings, & J. Kinzie (Eds.), *Using Evidence of Student Learning to Improve Higher Education* (pp. 146–159). San Francisco, CA: Jossey-Bass.

Eyler, J. (2009). The Power of Experiential Education. *Liberal Education, 95*(4), 24–31.

Felten, P., Barnett, B., & Fuller, J. (2014). Supporting Religious Pluralism at Elon University. *Diversity and Democracy, 17*(4), 23–24.

Felten, P., & Bauman, H.-D. L. (2013). Reframing Diversity and Student Engagement: Lessons from Deaf-Gain. In E. Dunne &

D. Owen (Eds.), *The Student Engagement Handbook: Practice in Higher Education* (pp. 267–278). Bingley, UK: Emerald.

Felten, P., & Clayton, P. H. (2011). Service-Learning. In W. Buskist & J. E. Groccia (Eds.), *Evidence-Based Teaching: New Directions for Teaching and Learning*, No. 128 (pp. 75–84). San Francisco, CA: Jossey-Bass.

Felten, P., & Finley, A. (2013). Motivating Teaching Excellence: Lessons from U.S. Teaching Awards. In D. J. Salter (Ed.), *Cases on Quality Teaching Practices in Higher Education* (pp. 228–238). Hershey, PA: IGI Global.

Fink, J. E., & Hummel, M. L. (2015). With Educational Benefits for All: Campus Inclusion Through Learning Communities Designed for Underserved Populations. In M. Benjamin (Ed.), *Learning Communities from Start to Finish: New Directions for Student Services*, No. 149 (pp. 29–40). San Francisco, CA: Jossey-Bass.

Fink, L. D. (2013). *Creating Significant Learning Experiences: An Integrated Approach to Designing College Courses*. San Francisco, CA: Jossey-Bass.

Finley, A., & McNair, T. (2013). *Assessing Underserved Students' Engagement in High-Impact Practices*. Washington, DC: Association for American Colleges and Universities.

Fisher, A., Demetriou, C., & Hall, D. (2013). Transfer United: Partnerships to Foster Transfer Student Success. In S. Whalen (Ed.), *Proceedings of the 9th National Symposium on Student Retention, 2013, San Diego* (pp. 522–531). Norman, OK: University of Oklahoma Press.

Flores, B. C., Becvar, J., Knaust, H., Lopez, J., & Tinajero, J. (n.d.). *Leadership Team. University of Texas at El Paso.* Retrieved August 4, 2015 from http://academics.utep.edu/Default.aspx?tabid=70272

Folsom, P., Yoder, F., & Joslin, J. E. (2015). *The New Advisor Guidebook: Mastering the Arts of Academic Advising.* San Francisco, CA: Jossey-Bass.

Freeman, S., Eddy, S. L., McDonough, M., Smith, M. K., Okoroafor, N., Jordt, H., & Wenderoth, M. P. (2014). Active Learning Increases Student Performance in Science, Engineering, and Mathematics. *Proceedings of the National Academy of Sciences, 111*(23), 8410–8415.

Gallup & Purdue University. (2014). *Great Jobs, Great Lives: The 2014 Gallup-Purdue Index Inaugural National Report.* Retrieved June 24, 2015 from http://products.gallup.com/168857/gallup-purdue-index-inaugural-national-report.aspx

Gawande, A. (2007). *Better: A Surgeon's Notes on Performance.* New York, NY: Picador.

Gayles, J. G., & Hu, S. (2009). The Influence of Student Engagement and Sport Participation in College Outcomes Among Division I Student Athletes. *Journal of Higher Education, 80*(3), 315–333.

Gee, J. P. (2003). *What Video Games Have to Teach Us About Learning and Literacy.* New York, NY: Palgrave Macmillan.

Georgetown University. (2015). Designing the Future(s) of the University. Retrieved September 1, 2015 from https://futures.georgetown.edu

Gigerenzer, G. (2014). *Risk Savvy: How to Make Good Decisions*. New York, NY: Viking.

Gonzaga University. (2015). Mission Statement and Statement of Affirmation. *About Gonzaga*. Retrieved April 15, 2015 from https://www.gonzaga.edu/about/mission/missionstatement.asp

Gose, B. (2014). How to Make Students' Campus Jobs More Meaningful. *Chronicle of Higher Education*, September 15. Retrieved December 17, 2014 from http://chronicle.com/article/How-to-Make-Students-Campus/148731/

Gurin, P., Nagda, B. A., & Lopez, G. E. (2004). The Benefits of Diversity in Education for Democratic Citizenship. *Journal of Social Issues*, *60*(1), 17–34.

Hakel, M. D. (1997). What We Must Learn from Alverno. *About Campus*, *2*(3), 16–21.

Hamon, A. (2012). Foundations of Excellence Efforts to Improve First-Year Experiences. *Purdue Today*. Retrieved September 1, 2015 from http://www.purdue.edu/newsroom/purduetoday/releases/2012/Q4/foundations-of-excellence-process-to-improve-first-year-experiences.html

Hartley, M., & Morphew, C. C. (2008). What's Being Sold and to What End? A Content Analysis of College Viewbooks. *Journal of Higher Education*, *79*(6), 671–691.

Hauhart, R. C., & Grahe, J. E. (2015). *Designing and Teaching Undergraduate Capstone Courses*. San Francisco, CA: Jossey-Bass.

Hensel, N. (Ed.). (2012). *Characteristics of Excellence in Undergraduate Research*. Washington, DC: Council on Undergraduate Research.

Hersh, R. H., & Merrow, J. (Eds.). (2005). *Declining by Degrees: Higher Education at Risk*. New York, NY: Palgrave Macmillan.

Higgings, M. C., & Kram, K. E. (2001). Reconceptualizing Mentoring at Work: A Developmental Perspective. *Academy of Management Review, 26*(2), 264–288.

Hrabowski, F. A., Suess, J. J., & Fritz, J. (2011). Assessment and Analytics in Institutional Transformation. *EDUCAUSE Review 46*(5), 15–28.

Huston, T. (2009). *Teaching What You Don't Know*. Cambridge, MA: Harvard University Press.

Hutchings, P., Huber, M. T., & Ciccone, A. (2011). *The Scholarship of Teaching and Learning Reconsidered: Institutional Integration and Impact*. San Francisco, CA: Jossey-Bass.

Ikenberry, S. O., & Kuh, G. D. (2015). From Compliance to Ownership: Why and How Colleges and Universities Assess Student Learning. In G. D. Kuh, S. O. Ikenberry, N. A. Jankowski, T. R. Cain, P. T. Ewell, P. Hutchings, & J. Kinzie (Eds.), *Using Evidence of Student Learning to Improve Higher Education* (pp. 1–23). San Francisco, CA: Jossey-Bass.

Johansson, C., & Felten, P. (2014). *Transforming Students: Fulfilling the Promise of Higher Education*. Baltimore, MD: Johns Hopkins University Press.

Johnson, W. B. (2007). *On Being a Mentor: A Guide for Higher Education Faculty*. New York, NY: Lawrence Erlbaum.

Jones, S. R., & Abes, E. S. (2013). *Identity Development of College Students: Advancing Frameworks for Multiple Dimensions of Identity*. San Francisco, CA: Jossey-Bass.

Jussim, L. (2013). Teachers' Expectations. In J. Hattie & E. Anderman (Eds.), *International Handbook of Student Achievement* (pp. 242–246). New York, NY: Routledge.

Keeling, R. P., & Hersh, R. H. (2012). *We're Losing Our Minds: Rethinking American Higher Education*. New York, NY: Palgrave Macmillan.

Kelchen, R. (2015). *The Landscape of Competency-Based Education: Enrollments, Demographics, and Affordability*. Washington, DC: Center on Higher Education Reform/American Enterprise Institute.

Keller, G. (2014). *Transforming a College: The Story of a Little-Known College's Climb to National Distinction* (2nd ed.). Baltimore, MD: Johns Hopkins University Press.

Kellogg Commission on the Future of State and Land-Grant Universities. (2000). *Returning to Our Roots: Toward a Coherent Campus Culture*, 5th Report. Washington, DC: National Association of State Universities and Land-Grant Colleges.

Kenney, D. R., Dumont, R., & Kenney, G. (2005). *Mission and Place: Strengthening Learning and Community Through Campus Design*. Westport, CT: Praeger.

Kezar, A. J., & Lester, J. (2011). *Enhancing Campus Capacity for Leadership: An Examination of Grassroots Leaders in Higher Education*. Stanford, CA: Stanford University Press.

Kiehn, J. (2015). Personal email communication with Charles Schroeder.

Klepfer, K., & Hull, J. (2012). *High School Rigor and Good Advice: Setting Up Students to Succeed.* Alexandria, VA: Center for Public Education, National School Boards Association.

Koch, S. S., Griffin, B. Q., & Barefoot, B. O. (2014). *National Survey of Student Success Initiatives at Two-Year Colleges.* Brevard, NC: John N. Gardner Institute for Excellence in Undergraduate Education. Retrieved December 17, 2014 from http://www.jngi.org/wordpress/wp-content/uploads/2014/07/National-2-yr-Survey-Booklet_webversion.pdf

Koedinger, K. R., Kim, J., Jia, J. Z., McLaughlin, E. A., & Bier, N. L. (2015). Learning Is Not a Spectator Sport: Doing Is Better Than Watching for Learning from a MOOC. *Proceedings of the Second (2015) ACM Conference on Learning at Scale.* New York, NY: ACM. Retrieved August 7, 2015 from http://dx.doi.org/10.1145/2724660.2724681

Koester, J., Hellenbrand, H., & Piper, T. D. (2008). The Challenge of Collaboration: Organizational Structure and Professional Identity. *About Campus, 13*(5), 12–19.

Kremer, G. (2013). Designing to Make a Difference: Authentic Integration of Professional Skills in an Engineering Capstone Design Course. In T. A. Ferrett, D. R. Geelan, W. M. Schlegel, & J. L. Steward (Eds.), *Connected Science: Strategies for Integrative Learning in College* (pp. 40–52). Bloomington, IN: Indiana University Press.

Kuh, G. D. (2008). *High-Impact Educational Practices: What They Are, Who Has Access to Them, and Why They Matter.* Washington, DC: Association of American Colleges and Universities.

Kuh, G. D., & Hutchings, P. (2015). Assessment and Initiative Fatigue: Keeping the Focus on Learning. In G. D. Kuh, S. O. Ikenberry, N. A. Jankowski, T. R. Cain, P. T. Ewell, P. Hutchings, & J. Kinzie (Eds.), *Using Evidence of Student Learning to Improve Higher Education* (pp. 183–200). San Francisco, CA: Jossey-Bass.

Kuh, G. D., Ikenberry, S. O., Jankowski, N. A., Cain, T. R., Ewell, P. T., Hutchings, P., & Kinzie, J. (Eds.) (2015). *Using Evidence of Student Learning to Improve Higher Education*. San Francisco, CA: Jossey-Bass.

Kuh, G. D., Kinzie, J., Schuh, J. H., Whitt, E. J., & Associates. (2010). *Student Success in College: Creating Conditions That Matter*. San Francisco, CA: Jossey-Bass.

Kurt, M. R., Olitsky, N. H., & Geis, P. J. (2013). Assessing Global Awareness over a Short-Term Study Abroad Sequence: A Factor Analysis. *Frontiers: Interdisciplinary Journal of Study Abroad, 23*, 22–41.

Lambert, L. M. (2015). A Grow Your Own Strategy to Develop Administrative Leadership. *Trusteeship*, March–April.

Lave, J. (1991). Situating Learning in Communities of Practice. *Perspectives on Socially Shared Cognition, 2*, 63–82.

Levin, H. M., & Garcia, E. (2013). Benefit-Cost Analysis of Accelerated Study in Associate Programs (ASAP) of the City University of New York (CUNY). *Center for the Benefit-Cost Studies in Education. Teachers College, Columbia University*. Retrieved on February 4, 2016 from http://cbcse.org/wordpress/wpcontent/uploads/2013/05/Levin_ASAP_Benefit_Cost_Report_FINAL_05222013.pdf

Levin, H. M., Garcia, E., & Morgan, J. (2012). Cost-Effectiveness of Accelerated Study in Associate Programs (ASAP) of the City University of New York (CUNY). *Center for Benefit-Cost Studies of Education, Columbia University Teachers College.* Retrieved on February 4, 2016 from www.cuny.edu/academics/programs/notable/asap/Levin_Report_WEB.pdf

Light, R. J. (2001). *Making the Most of College: Students Speak Their Minds.* Cambridge, MA: Harvard University Press.

Linderman, D. (2016). Personal telephone interview with Leo Lambert. February 3, 2016.

Maki, P. L. (2010). *Assessing for Learning: Building a Sustainable Commitment Across the Institution* (2nd ed.). Sterling, VA: Stylus.

Marquardt, M. (2005). *Leading with Questions: How Leaders Find the Right Solutions by Knowing What to Ask.* San Francisco, CA: Jossey-Bass.

Mazur, E. (2009). Farewell, Lecture? *Science, 323,* 50–51.

McNair, T. B., & Albertine, S. (2012). Seeking High-Quality, High-Impact Learning: The Imperative of Faculty Development and Curricular Intentionality. *Peer Review, 14*(3), 4–5.

MDRC (2014). New Study Shows CUNY's ASAP Program Boosts Two-Year Graduation Rate of Community College Students Who Need Remedial Education. New York: MDRC. Retrieved on February 6, 2016 from http://www.mdrc.org/news/press-release/cuny%E2%80%99s-asap-program-boosts-graduation-rate-students-who-need-remedial-education

Mehaffy, G. L. (2015). *Re-Imagining the First Year of College*. Conference on the First-Year Experience, Dallas, TX. February 7–10, 2015.

Mellow, G. (2014). Telephone interview with Leo Lambert. December 2, 2014.

Mentkowski, M., & Associates. (2000). *Learning That Lasts: Integrating Learning, Development, and Performance in College and Beyond*. San Francisco, CA: Jossey-Bass.

Michael, J. M., & Dueer, V. (2014). *Adventure West Virginia Assessment*. Morgantown, WV: West Virginia University Office of Institutional Research.

Miller, M. D. (2014). *Minds Online: Teaching Effectively with Technology*. Cambridge, MA: Harvard University Press.

Miller, P. (2015). Personal interview with Leo Lambert. February 6, 2015.

Miller, T. E., Bender, B. E., Schuh, J. H., & Associates. (2005). *Promoting Reasonable Expectations: Aligning Student and Institutional Views of the College Experience*. San Francisco, CA: Jossey-Bass.

Morrill, R. L. (2007). *Strategic Leadership: Integrating Strategy and Leadership in Colleges and Universities*. New York, NY: Rowman & Littlefield/American Council on Education.

National Center for Education Statistics. (2015). *Institutional Retention and Graduation Rates for Undergraduate Students*. Retrieved October 1, 2015 from http://nces.ed.gov/programs/coe/indicator_cva.asp

National Survey of Student Engagement. (2014). *Bringing the Institution into Focus—Annual Results 2014.* Bloomington, IN: Indiana Center for Postsecondary Research.

National Survey of Student Engagement. (2015). *Engagement Insights: Survey Findings on the Quality of Undergraduate Education—Annual Results 2015.* Bloomington, IN: Indiana University Center for Postsecondary Research.

Newman, L. E., Carpenter, S., Grawe, N., & Jaret-McKinstry, S. (2015). Creating a Culture Conducive to Integrative Learning. *Peer Review, 16–17*(4–1).

Newton, F. B., & Ender, S. C. (2010). *Students Helping Students: A Guide for Peer Educators on College Campuses* (2nd ed.). San Francisco, CA: Jossey-Bass.

Noel-Levitz. (2010). *Enhancing Student Success by Treating "Student Jobs" as "Real Jobs": Noel-Levitz White Paper* Coralville, IA: Noel-Levitz Retrieved on November 30, 2015 from https://www.ruffalonl.com/papers-research-higher-education-fundraising/2010/enhancing-student-success-student-jobs

Nowacek, R. S. (2011). *Agents of Integration: Understanding Transfer as a Rhetorical Act.* Carbondale, IL: Illinois State University Press.

Nowicki, S., & Baker, L. D. (2015). Personal interview with Leo Lambert. February 25, 2015.

O'Donnell, K. (2013). Bringing HIPs to Scale: Turning Good Practice into Lasting Policy. In G. D. Kuh & K. O'Donnell (Eds.), *Ensuring Quality and Taking High-Impact Practices to*

Scale (pp. 15–22). Washington, DC: Association of American Colleges and Universities.

O'Meara, K., Terosky, A. L., & Neumann, A. (2008). Faculty Careers and Work Lives: A Professional Growth Prospective. *ASHE Higher Education Report, 34*(3), 1–221.

Palmer, M. S., Bach, D. J., & Streifer, A. S. (2014). Measuring the Promise: A Learning-Focused Syllabus Rubric. *To Improve the Academy, 33*(1), 14–36.

Parks, S. D. (2011). *Big Questions, Worthy Dreams: Mentoring Emerging Adults in Their Search for Meaning, Purpose, and Faith,* 10th anniversary edition. San Francisco, CA: Jossey-Bass.

Pascarella, E. T., & Terenzini, P. T. (2005). *How College Affects Students: A Third Decade of Research.* San Francisco, CA: Jossey-Bass.

Patel, E. (2014). *Remarks at the Fourth Annual President's Interfaith and Community Service Campus Challenge.* George Washington University, Washington, DC, September 23.

Pierce, S. R. (2014). *Governance Reconsidered: How Boards, Presidents, Administrators, and Faculty Can Help Their Colleges Thrive.* San Francisco, CA: Jossey-Bass.

Pike, G. R., Hansen, M. J., & Childress, J. E. (2014). The Influence of Students' Pre-College Characteristics, High School Experiences, College Expectations, and Initial Enrollment Characteristics on Degree Attainment. *Journal of College Student Retention, 16*(1), 1–23.

Radjou, N., & Prabhu, J. (2014). *Frugal Innovation: How to Do More with Less.* New York, NY: PublicAffairs.

Ray, J., & Kafka, S. (2014). Life in College Matters for Life After College: New Gallup-Purdue Study Looks at Links among College, Work, and Well-Being. *Gallup Poll*, May 6. Retrieved December 17, 2014 from http://www.gallup.com/poll/168848/life-college-matters-life-college.aspx

Rollins College. (2015). Wall of WOW. Retrieved June 25, 2015 from http://www.rollins.edu/service-excellence/wall-of-wow/index.html

Rosenthal, R., &. Jacobson, L. (1966). Teachers' Expectancies: Determinants of Pupils' IQ Gains. *Psychological Reports*, *19*(1), 115–118.

Rosenthal, R., &. Jacobson, L. (1968). *Pygmalion in the Classroom: Teacher Expectation and Pupils' Intellectual Development.* New York, NY: Holt, Rinehart and Winston.

Samhat, N. H. (2013). *Opening Convocation.* Wofford College. Retrieved June 25, 2015 from http://www.wofford.edu/president/OpeningConvocation2013/

Schilling, K. M., & Schilling, K. L. (1999). Increasing Expectations for Student Effort. *About Campus*, *4*(2), 4–10.

Schilling, K. M., & Schilling, K. L. (2005). Expectations and Performance. In M. L. Upcraft, J. N. Gardner, & B. O. Barefoot (Eds.), *Challenging and Supporting the First-Year Student: A Handbook for Improving the First Year of College* (pp. 108–124). San Francisco, CA: Jossey-Bass.

Schroeder, C. (1999). Forging Educational Partnerships That Advance Student Learning. In G. S. Blimling & E. J. Whitt (Eds.), *Good Practice in Student Affairs: Principles to*

Foster Student Learning (pp. 133–156). San Francisco, CA: Jossey-Bass.

Schroeder, C. (2001). The Mystery Shopper Program: An Innovative Tool for Assessing Performance. In R. L. Swing (Ed.), *Proving and Improving: Strategies for Assessing the First College Year*, No. 33 (pp. 75–79). Columbia, SC: University of South Carolina, National Resource Center for the First-Year Experience and Students in Transition.

Schroeder, C. (2012). Personal observation at Northwestern Louisiana State University.

Schroeder, C. (2013). Reframing Retention Strategy: A Focus on Process. In D. H. Kalsbeek (Ed.), *Reframing Retention Strategies for Institutional Improvement, New Directions for Higher Education*, No. 161 (pp. 39–47). San Francisco, CA: Jossey-Bass.

Schroeder, C. C., & Shushok, F. (2015). An Interview with Charles C. Schroeder. *About Campus*, *20*(1), 13–19.

Scrivener, S., Weiss, M. J., Ratledge, A., Rudd, T., Sommo, C., & Fresques, H. (2015). *Doubling Graduation Rates: Three-Year Effects of CUNY's Accelerated Study in Associate Programs (ASAP) for Developmental Education Students*. New York, NY: MDRC. Retrieved from http://www.mdrc.org/sites/default/files/doubling_graduation_rates_fr.pdf

Seattle University. (n.d.). *Collegia Program*. Retrieved from https://www.seattleu.edu/cotp/collegia/

Selingo, J. J. (2013). *College (Un)bound: The Future of Higher Education and What it Means for Students*. New York, NY: Houghton Mifflin.

Senge, P. (1990). *The Fifth Discipline: The Art and Practice of the Learning Organization.* New York, NY: Doubleday.

Seymour, D. (2002). *Once Upon a Campus: Lessons for Improving Quality and Productivity in Higher Education.* Westport, CT: American Council on Education / Oryx Press.

Shulman, L. S. (1993). Teaching as Community Property: Putting an End to Pedagogical Solitude. *Change, 25*(6), 6–7.

Silverman, S. C., Aliabadi, S., & Stiles, M. R. (2014). Meeting the Needs of Commuter, Part-Time, Transfer, and Returning Students. In S. J. Quaye & S. R. Harper (Eds.), *Student Engagement in Higher Education: Theoretical Perspectives and Practical Approaches for Diverse Populations* (2nd ed.), (pp. 223–242). New York, NY: Routledge.

Slaughter, G., & Rhoades, G. (2004). *Academic Capitalism and the New Economy: Markets, State, and Higher Education.* Baltimore, MD: Johns Hopkins University Press.

Spector, J. (2012, September 11). Dissolving the Classroom Walls. *Chronicle,* Retrieved September 14, 2015 from http://www.dukechronicle.com/article/2012/09/dissolving-classroom-walls

Steele, C. M. (1997). A Threat in the Air: How Stereotypes Shape Intellectual Identity and Performance. *American Psychologist, 52*(6), 613–629.

Steele, C. M. (2010). *Whistling Vivaldi and Other Clues to How Stereotyping Affects Us.* New York, NY: W.W. Norton and Company.

Stevens, C. J., D'Angelo, B., Rennell, N., Muzyka, D., Pannabecker, V., & Maid, B. (2014). Implementing a Writing Course in an Online RN-BSN Program. *Nurse Educator*, *39*(1), 17–21.

Strayhorn, T. L. (2012). *College Students' Sense of Belonging: A Key to Educational Success for All Students*. New York, NY: Routledge.

Study Group on the Conditions of Excellence in American Higher Education. (1984). *Involvement in Learning: Realizing the Potential of American Higher Education*. Washington, DC: National Institute of Education.

Sullivan, D. F. (2015). The Sustainable College: Thriving and Serving the Nation in the 21st Century. *Trusteeship Magazine*. Retrieved on June 24, 2015, from http://agb.org/trusteeship/2015/mayjune/the-sustainable-college-thriving-and-serving-the-nation-in-the-21st-century

Sullivan, W. M., & Rosin, M. S. (2008). *A New Agenda for Higher Education: Shaping a Life of the Mind for Practice*. San Francisco, CA: Jossey-Bass.

Summers, M. F., & Hrabowski III, F. A. (2006). Preparing Minority Scientists and Engineers. *Science*, *311*, 1870–1871.

Tagg, J. (2003). *The Learning Paradigm College*. San Francisco, CA: Anker/Jossey-Bass.

Treisman, U. (1992). Studying Students Studying Calculus: A Look at the Lives of Minority Mathematics Students in College. *College Mathematics Journal*, *23*(5), 362–372.

Tough, P. (2014, May 18). Who Gets to Graduate? *New York Times Magazine*, 26–33, 41–42, 54, 56.

Townsley, E., Packard, B. W., & Paus, E. (2015). Making the Lynk at Mount Holyoke: Institutionalizing Integrative Learning. *Peer Review, 16*, 26–29.

Trible, P. (2015) Personal correspondence with Leo Lambert. December 17, 2014.

University of Louisville. (2015). *Paul Weber Award for Departmental Excellence in Teaching*. Retrieved August 7, 2015 from http://louisville.edu/delphi/awards/paulweber

University of Michigan. (2015). *Undergraduate Research Opportunity Program, Evaluation and Assessment*. Retrieved June 24, 2015 from http://www.lsa.umich.edu/urop/aboutus/evaluationassessment

University of Missouri. (2015). Enhancing the Mizzou Student Dining Experience. *Campus Dining Services*. Retrieved April 15, 2015 from http://dining.missouri.edu/about/

University of New Mexico. (2015). *Graduation Project*. Retrieved June 25, 2015 from http://success.unm.edu/grad-project/

University of Notre Dame. (2015). *The Point of It All*. Retrieved June 24, 2015 from http://firstyear.nd.edu/parents/the-point-of-it-all/

University of South Carolina. (2015). *Carolinian Creed*. Retrieved April 15, 2015 from http://www.sa.sc.edu/creed/

Vandermaas-Peeler, M. (2015). Personal interview with Leo Lambert. February 12, 2015.

Vice President for Student Life, University of Iowa. (n.d.). *Iowa GROW*. Retrieved June 22, 2015 from https://vp.studentlife.uiowa.edu/initiatives/grow/

Wabash College. (2015). Rule of Conduct. *Academic Bulletin Rule of Conduct—2014-2015*. Retrieved June 22, 2015 from http://www.wabash.edu/bulletin/home.cfm?site_code_id=971

Wake Forest University. (2010). *Living Our Values: Administrative Report, Office of the President*. Retrieved June 25, 2015 from http://president.wfu.edu/living-our-values-administrative-report/

Walvoord, B. E. (2010). *Assessment Clear and Simple: A Practical Guide for Institutions, Departments, and General Education*. (2nd ed.). San Francisco, CA: Jossey-Bass.

Wardle, E. (2007). Understanding Transfer from FYC: Preliminary Results of a Longitudinal Study. *WPA Journal, 31*(1–2), 65–85.

Weaver, K. (2015). Trophies, Treasure, and Turmoil: College Athletics at a Tipping Point. *Change, 47*(1), 36–45.

Weick, K.E. (1983). Contradictions in a community of scholars: The cohesion–accuracy tradeoff. *Review of Higher Education, 20*, 23–33.

Wieman, C., Perkins, K., & Gilbert, S. (2010). Transforming Science Education at Large Research Universities: A Case Study in Progress. *Change, 42*(2), 6–14.

Winkelmes, M.-A. (2013). Transparency in Teaching: Faculty Share Data and Improve Students' Learning. *Liberal Education, 99*(2). Retrieved September 22, 2015 from http://www.aacu.org/publications-research/periodicals/transparency-teaching-faculty-share-data-and-improve-students

Wolf-Wendel, L., Ward, K., & Kinzie, J. (2009). A Tangled Web of Terms: The Overlap and Unique Contribution of Involvement, Engagement, and Integration to Understanding College Student Success. *Journal of College Student Development, 50*(4), 407–428.

Yamada, H. (2014). *Community College Pathways' Program Success: Assessing the First Two Years' Effectiveness of Statway.* Stanford, CA: Carnegie Foundation for the Advancement of Teaching.

Yasso, T. J. (2005). Whose Culture Has Capital? *Race, Ethnicity, and Education, 8*(1), 69–91.

A

CORE THEMES AND ACTION PRINCIPLES

Learning Matters: Action Principles (Chapter 2)

1. Take institutional responsibility for student learning.

2. Create opportunities for learning in and out of the classroom.

3. Recognize the complexity of meaningful learning.

4. Help students integrate learning experiences.

5. Promote and reward learning for everyone at the institution.

Relationships Matter: Action Principles (Chapter 3)

1. Make relationships central to learning.

2. Create pathways to lead students into relationships with peers, faculty, and staff.

3. Nurture both learning and belonging through relationships.

4. Encourage everyone on campus to cultivate relationships.

5. Celebrate and reward relationship building.

Expectations Matter: Action Principles (Chapter 4)

1. Focus expectations on what matters most to student learning and success.
2. Communicate, and reiterate, high expectations.
3. Set expectations early.
4. Implement policies and practices congruent with espoused expectations.
5. Help individuals and groups develop the capacity to set and meet their own expectations.

Alignment Matters: Action Principles (Chapter 5)

1. Make alignment a shared goal.
2. Align administrative practices and policies.
3. Align academic programs and campus practices.
4. Challenge students to align their learning.
5. Leverage the benefits of alignment.

Improvement Matters: Action Principles (Chapter 6)

1. Recognize that assessment is fundamental to improvement.
2. Focus assessment on improving what matters most.

3. Commit to using evidence to inform changes.

4. Involve everyone in the process of making change.

5. Adapt best practices from elsewhere.

6. Cultivate an ethos of positive restlessness.

7. Model the process of improvement for students and the institution.

Leadership Matters: Action Principles (Chapter 7)

1. Lead through collaborative practices.

2. Articulate clear, aspirational goals linked to institutional mission and values.

3. Cultivate a culture that keeps students and learning at the center of decision making.

4. Foster shared responsibility and leadership at all levels of the institution.

5. Make strategic choices and take informed risks.

6. Focus on dynamic, improvement-oriented planning, executing, and communicating.

B

QUESTIONS FOR REFLECTION

Learning Matters (Chapter 2)

1. What is your role in student learning at your institution? How do you, and your institution, measure your effectiveness? What areas for improvement do you see in your efforts? What can you do to be more effective?

2. What pedagogies or programs at your institution create engaging and integrated learning? How can you make these programs even more effective? How can you make these programs available to more students?

3. How do you currently, or how might you, use the essential elements of high-impact practices to develop powerful learning experiences for students both in and outside the classroom?

4. Where is integrative learning most likely to occur at your campus? What could you do to support more integrative learning for students, faculty, and staff?

5. How does your institution, and how do you, respond to struggle and failure? What can you do to create a climate where failure can be a step toward learning? What actions can you take to incorporate this way of thinking into your own work and into programs and systems at your institution?

6. How is learning promoted and rewarded for faculty and staff at your institution? What are some creative new ways that learning could be supported?

7. What can you do to learn more and to contribute more to your peers' learning?

Relationships Matter (Chapter 3)

1. How does your institution create structures, environments, and programs to encourage meaningful relationships? Who do these structures and programs tend to involve, and who typically is not included? What could be done to broaden and expand participation beyond these individuals and groups?

2. Are there systemic organizational barriers on your campus that inhibit an integrated approach to relationship building?

3. Which programs and practices best foster the development of strong relationships between students and faculty on your campus? What programs at other institutions might work on your campus?

4. What are the most important and effective practices your institution uses to encourage healthy interactions between students and their peers?

5. Are meaningful relationships with students integrated in areas across your institution such as academic affairs, athletics, and student life or through supervision of student employment?

6. How are positive relationships supported, rewarded, and recognized on your campus?

Expectations Matter (Chapter 4)

1. What are the expectations that your institution explicitly communicates to students, faculty, and staff? What are the implicit expectations the institution communicates? How do the explicit and implicit expectations align?

2. How clear, consistent, coherent, and explicit are expectations for different constituent groups (that is, students, staff, faculty) at your institution? How are those expectations linked to your institution's mission and values and focused on students and learning? Where and how are these communicated?

3. Are expectations for student performance set at appropriately high levels, given students' academic preparation? Are academic challenges for students balanced with appropriate support?

4. How do you and your institution encourage and support individuals and groups in setting and meeting their own expectations?

5. What methods (for example, honor codes, traditions, rituals, formal events, trainings, social media) does your institution use to uphold, reinforce, and celebrate expectations?

6. How do you address gaps between desired institutional expectations and actual performance?

Alignment Matters (Chapter 5)

1. To what extent are curriculum, policies, structures, and resources aligned with your institution's aspirations for undergraduate education? To what extent are your own work and values aligned with your institution's aspirations?

2. Which leaders at your institution are asking hard questions about alignment? Who else could and should be working toward alignment?

3. Do you engage in environmental assessments to identify dysfunctional and misaligned processes? If so, when and how does this work best? If not, how might you begin?

4. How often does your institution challenge prevailing assumptions and take reasonable risks to improve cross-functional processes and programs? How can systems thinking enable your institution to connect the parts to create a better, more holistic experience for students?

5. Are your major institutional processes, such as enrollment and advising, relatively smooth and seamless, or are they misaligned? How effective are the handoffs between key stakeholders in critical process areas?

6. How can you enhance the design and implementation of policies and practices so that they are seamless and agile not only for students, but also for staff, faculty, and other key stakeholders?

7. What are the barriers to better alignment on your campus? How can you cultivate perspectives and relationships that will make alignment more possible in the future?

Improvement Matters (Chapter 6)

1. How would you describe your institution's culture of assessment and improvement? How much does accreditation drive your assessment work?

2. What examples can you identify of evidence-informed action at your institution? What lessons can you draw from those examples for your next improvement efforts?

3. How (and with whom) are you sharing, on and beyond your campus, both the processes and the results of your improvement efforts?

4. How can you involve more stakeholders, including students and faculty, in improvement initiatives on your campus?

5. How can you and your institution most effectively model the improvement process for students?

6. How do you and your institution support professional development to help people and groups be more capable of using assessment for improvement?

7. How are you and your institution replicating, celebrating, and rewarding successful improvement efforts?

Leadership Matters (Chapter 7)

1. How does your institution cultivate leadership at all levels? Do you have programs for how to engage students, alumni, and others in leadership on campus?

2. How can you enhance shared responsibility for leadership at your institution?

3. What are some specific examples of ways that institutional values and priorities guide leadership and decision making in your context?

4. When do you and other leaders on your campus take strategic risks? Who are the leaders on campus who are most likely to take risks? What have you and your colleagues learned from these experiences with risk taking?

5. Does your program and campus have a strategic planning and resource allocation process in place that is linked to your campus vision of what matters most for student learning and success?

6. How does your institution determine its highest priorities? How does learning factor into these priorities?

C

PROGRAMS AND INSTITUTIONS PROFILED IN THE BOOK

Chapter 1: What Matters Most

Chapter 2: Learning Matters

Reacting to the Past games
Page 17

Mount Holyoke College

Making the Lynk initiative
Page 23

University of Iowa

Iowa GROW (Guided Reflection on Work) program
Page 24

California State University System

Give Students a Compass project
Page 28

Cosumnes River College (CRC)
Page 28

Sacramento State University
Page 28

University of Michigan

Undergraduate Research Opportunity Program
(UROP)
Page 29

University of North Carolina at Chapel Hill

Transfer United (TU)
Page 29

Northern Arizona University

First-Year Learning Initiative (FYLI)
Page 32

Chapter 3: Relationships Matter

Chapter 4: Expectations Matter

University of Houston (UH)

UH in 4 program
   Page 82

Lynchburg College
   Page 82

Hendrix College
   Page 82

Tennessee Tech Centers
   Page 82

San Diego State University
   Page 82

Duke University
   Page 82

Complete College America (CCA)
   Page 83

University of New Mexico

The Graduation Project
   Page 83

University of Nevada at Las Vegas

Transparency in Teaching and Learning in Higher
Education project
   Page 85

Georgia Institute of Technology (Georgia Tech)
   Page 86

Chapter 5: Alignment Matters

Chapter 6: Improvement Matters

Western Interstate Collegiate Commission for Higher Education (WICHE)

Passport Project

American Association of Colleges & Universities (AAC&U) Liberal Education and America's Promise (LEAP) Essential Learning Outcomes (ELOs)

AAC&U Valid Assessment of Learning in Undergraduate Education (VALUE) rubrics
    Page 123

Multistate Collaborative Assessment Initiative (MCAI)
    Page 123

Hope College
    Page 124

University of Maryland, Baltimore County
    Page 124

University of California—Merced

Students Assessing Teaching and Learning program
    Page 125

University of Exeter

Students as Change Agents program
    Page 126

University of Missouri-Columbia
    Pages 120, 127

University of Washington (UW)
    Page 127

Gallaudet University

DeafSpace
    Page 129

Chapter 7: Leadership Matters

Alverno College
Page 146

Bryn Mawr College

Students as Learners and Teachers (SaLT) program
Page 147

Haverford College

Students as Learners and Teachers (SaLT) program
Page 147

Elon University

Faculty administrative fellows program
Page 149

Bucknell University

Executive intern program, task force on student campus experience
Pages 149, 150

Duke University

Intellectual Climate Committee
Page 153

DePaul University

Alumni Sharing Knowledge (ASK) program
Page 154

James Madison University
Page 154

Stella and Charles Guttman Community College
Page 155

Miami Dade College
Page 156

D

ACCESSING THIS BOOK'S ONLINE MATERIALS

We have created a website to support your use of this book for retreats, courses, and discussions. On that site you will find resources you may use including print-ready handouts and presentation-ready slides with the Core Themes, Action Principles, and Questions for Reflection. The site also has short video interviews that elaborate on the book, and other helpful resources.

www.TheUndergraduateExperience.org

INDEX